Couples

East Hampton, New York 1983

Willem de Kooning Artist

Artist Elaine de Kooning

Couples
Speaking from the Heart

Photographs by Mariana Cook

Introduction by Paul Ricoeur

CHRONICLE BOOKS

SAN FRANCISCO

Printed in Italy

Library of Congress Cataloging-in-Publication Data
available.
ISBN: 0-8118-2874-3(PB)
ISBN: 0-8118-2873-5(HC)

Book and cover design: David Valentine

Distributed in Canada by Raincoast Books
9050 Shaughnessy Street
Vancouver, BC V6P 6E5

10 9 8 7 6 5 4 3 2 1

Chronicle Books LLC
85 Second Street
San Francisco, CA 94105

www.chroniclebooks.com

To the wind

Carmel, California 1994

May Weiss Retired Medical Technician

Retired Medical Technician Stanley Weiss

Contents

INTRODUCTION

Paul Ricoeur

It is a pleasure to have before one's eyes the new volume of photographs by Mariana Cook. Those who know her earlier collections, *Mothers and Sons* and *Fathers and Daughters,* will first be struck by the astounding variety of human relationships that are formed in a couple. You do not choose either your parent or your child, but in a couple you are considered to have chosen your partner. This is the first thought that springs to mind. Upon reflection, you see that the couples presented here offer a greater enigma than the family tie, precisely because the relationship is not prescribed by nature. It is open to a range of experimentation that society has not succeeded in controlling.

The bonds of the couple are at once vaster and more secret than those of the family. Vaster, they are indeed: you have married couples and unmarried couples, gay and lesbian pairs, even simple friends, almost brothers and sisters. The degree of intimacy remains very mysterious not only to others, but even to those who live together and form what we commonly call "a couple." What mixture of chance, necessity, and free choice lies concealed behind this simple word: couples?

It is precisely the function of the photograph, accompanied by the story of a life, to pierce a little through the couple's layer of secrecy—although the conjunction of image and text may only make it still more impenetrable. Before saying a word about the relation between the photograph and the narrative, let me emphasize the centrality of the photograph, and even more than the photograph itself, the central role of the photographer. It is she, Mariana Cook, who has accepted the diversity of the human situations represented here. She has received these couples the way they wished to be seen—in their clothing, in their physical attitude. She has respected the precise distance between the individuals. Behind the eye of the camera, there was another eye, a benevolent gaze, which,

far from capturing the image, wished to return it to the individuals. The image is not stolen or taken from them without their knowledge; it is given to be seen, to assist in the life story. Yes, in these images there is a great generosity, a great care taken to include both the image and the story behind it with the desire to understand.

If the photograph is the work of an artist, seen through the artist's gaze, the narratives written or told by the very persons who are photographed are flung onto paper with no particular art: they are too close, too familiar, sometimes too conventional, often too simple, although not self-indulgent. Where the text may seem too personal the photograph appears to lend distance.

Something indeed occurs between the photograph and the text, between the photograph given to be seen and the text given to be read. Apart from the difference in perspective, differing relations to space and time give rise to subtle dialogues between the picture and the narrative. On the one hand, the photograph exists entirely in space. All its points are simultaneous; no prescribed order is imposed on reading the image. As for time, the photograph is instantaneous. Its contact with time is that of the opening of the camera's lens. We do not know whether the image sums up a life or if it catches a fleeting moment. Raising the question refers us to the accompanying text. The text, unlike the image, unfolds in time; it recounts a story. Often it tells how these things began—what chance determined the birth of the couple; what vicissitudes, and sometimes trials, these two lives have been through; how long the union has existed, what agreement has resulted with time; at the price of what concessions, what silences, what quarrels, what patience. The narrative also tells, although not always and even not often, what life is like outside the couple, away from the intimate world; at work, at the office, the factory, at the head of a company, in the whirlwind of professions, in the privacy of a business meeting, a medical office. Professional life, however, is but a detour leading back to the intimacy of the couple. This is where the large questions emerge.

What is the meaning of all this? Is there a meaning? What does it mean to be a man, to be a woman, a man for a woman, a woman for a man, a woman for a woman, a man for a man? What is love? Is it as strong as death? The partners question. Those whose liaison society disapproves of seek to justify themselves, and the photograph expresses their quest for recognition, their protest, their demands. It is in this way that the text refers to the image, the life story to the photograph. What, then, takes place between the narrative and the photograph?

We first believe that narrative goes further than the image, which is silent. But is it not also true that words can conceal rather than reveal? The power of the image is precisely to exhibit, to uncover, to open, however unconsciously, what the text closes up. Even the most carefully selected dress or, on the contrary, the most careless, the most casual, shows us something of which the subject is unaware. And then there are the uncovered, naked parts of the body; the face, the hands. The face explores the entire being; it reveals an interior, it is defenseless. As for the hands, they don't always know how to hold themselves, where to put themselves: to hide? to flutter? settle on a shoulder, around a neck? to join? to clasp? The hands unwittingly express the failure of the very control that the narrative attempts to impose on life. There is even a couple stripped of all clothing; their nakedness is eloquent, not immodest, exposed without shame, against a background of garden, a background of paradise, with the visible promise of a little human carried high in the fertile belly. But, in the end, nudity conceals the secret of a relationship no less than the most carefully arranged clothing. Every life shown is also a life concealed, whether exposed in the instant by the photograph or spelled out in time by the narrative.

What remains an enigma is the link between two lives. It is here that the narrative and the photograph are the most discordant, accumulating their respective deficiencies as well as their expressive power. The narrative seeks to blend together two stories, to weave one into the other, but it cannot. The attempt to mingle two lives has something desperate about it. What then does the photograph do? It allows a gap between two bodies. Never does it show their union, their fusion. The discretion of the image protects what remains discrete, secret, in the most complete accord between two lives. Observe the void gaping between the bodies, the pure space against which the bodies stand out: Sometimes it is a natural setting, rarely is it a tool, or an instrument—some object that would recall the social connection and hide the profound solitude of beings; it is most often a black band between the bodies, a dark background behind them. This gap signifies the history that is lacking in the instantaneousness of the image. It signifies the backdrop that no life story can ever exhaust. It protects the secret of each life, the secret of each union. It says without saying what is inextricable.

In the end, the photograph and the narrative join together in the same question: Why are these two people together? What does it mean to be together? The gratitude of this privileged reader goes to her who is the master-builder of this confrontation and of these exchanges between image and word.

Mariana Cook Photographer
Art Dealer Hans P. Kraus, Jr.

In 1983, I was commissioned by a rare-book dealer to photograph two of his colleagues, Hanni and Hans Kraus. It was one of my first private commissions and I did not have the professional discretion, when asked if I would like to take a swim in their pool, to say no. Mrs. Kraus lent me a bathing suit. Mr. Kraus telephoned their son.

Later that evening, I met Hans Peter Kraus, Jr., then twenty-five. He was a specialist in nineteenth-century photographs and also owned some early photographs made by my mentor, Ansel Adams. Hans was tall, dark, and handsome with lively eyes and a mustache that concealed his mischievous smile. We fell in love immediately. We saw one another for months, but we were too young. We parted, but kept in touch. No hard feelings.

Seven years passed, and one evening my father took me to the black-tie annual meeting of the Morgan Library. Hans was there with his mother. We were the only two people in the room under seventy. We were pleased to see each other and said we'd call one another the next day to make a theater date. A month later, when I remembered I'd forgotten to call him, I left a message. He called back three weeks later. He bought the theater tickets. I was to take him to dinner.

We enjoyed the play, and dinner, but when I attempted to pay the bill with a credit card, I was informed that the restaurant only took cash. Hans told me I owed him dinner and the theater. We began again, and were married sixteen months later.

I thought I'd finished making all the pictures for this book when my editor asked me to include a self-portrait with my husband. The thought had occurred to me previously, but I wasn't sure how to portray such a personal union. I dreaded it; but as with the other pictures in this book, I was curious to explore what might be revealed. Our four-year-old daughter, Emily, wanted to be in the picture with her bear, which wasn't what I'd visualized. I had composed the photograph from the knees up. We suggested that she sit on the floor. "But the camera won't see me if I do that," Emily said. I found a solution. I put a short cable release on the camera which required Emily's help in clicking the shutter. "Now," I'd say. Sometimes she clicked right away. Other times, she gave instructions and clicked when she felt like it. It's all in the timing.

Mariana Cook

My father called. "I have a girl here for you to meet. She has a great figure and is a pupil of Ansel Adams. She's swimming in the pool."

Still rebellious, I would hardly have sought my father's advice in social matters. The enthusiasm of his introduction, though, caught me off guard on a rainy Saturday afternoon in April, so I invited Mariana Cook over to see my Ansel Adams collection. She liked the parmelian prints and I admired her unconventional free spirit and her obsessive quest for truth and the secret of life.

After a passionate four-month relationship, I found myself petrified about uttering the word "love." Mimi was happiest in her darkroom. In fact, the making of analytical portraits has been her primary vehicle for pursuing truth. Neither of us was ready to settle down. We parted company.

Eight years later, my father having passed away in the interim, we reconnected. I had never been able to get Mimi out of my heart and instinct told me that if we ever got together again, I would be hooked. We dated for a year and the "L" word began tripping off my tongue. Still, she refused to live with me without a commitment. So I made one!

I am lucky to be married to the woman I love. Together, I believe that we have discovered the secret of life: our daughter, Emily.

Hans Kraus

Tom Maley Sculptor

Child Psychologist Helen Maley

Sometimes we've had little quarrels in our sixty-two years of married life. I would get mad occasionally when Helen came up with a provable right answer. I always demanded proof. I'd get mad for a short time until I got over it by telling myself I could be wrong sometimes.

What makes a marriage work is respect and just plain old love. Those ingredients are simple to figure out. The fact that neither one of us was short financially helped, too. Having children is the biggest challenge. It drew us together because we were both equally responsible. Helen was an expert in early childhood, so that helped us to begin with, but it's hard. It takes a lot of your time and there's a lot to worry about.

Our marriage has been pretty uneventful and pleasant in general. We are lucky. A lot of people aren't.

Tom Maley

I was heartsick when I didn't score high enough on my college board exams to get into Vassar. But it was the luckiest thing that ever happened to me because I ended up at Pembroke and Tom was at neighboring Brown University, which was a very interesting place to be.

An English professor and his wife invited Tom and me for tea one afternoon. They were both delightful people. They also asked two others. I didn't go off with Tom right away because he was tall, and the other gentleman was short, so we were paired. Pretty soon, Tom got around to calling me. That was very nice.

We were madly in love for a long time before we actually got married. We decided to get married, even though it was against college rules. The rules were set up to get girls to do the wrong things, if you want to call them the wrong things. They made rules about when you came back in at night, so girls didn't say they'd gone out and then they couldn't come back; all these puritanical, crazy rules. We were so young and so naive.

How would I describe Tom? That's a big and wonderful question. He has a very unique personality. He's very sure of himself and he's not a bit sure of himself. He's almost absurdly modest and he's sometimes just as absurdly not modest. He's got a very good sense of humor and he's very kind. He's special.

We are lucky because we grew together. It takes forever to grow together. It's a lifetime career! It's a matter of luck.

Helen Maley

Alan Greenspan Central Banker
Journalist Andrea Mitchell

We have been best friends for a long time, but even so, our marriage in 1996 has brought many unexpected blessings. To those who don't know us, we are perhaps an unlikely couple. He is a mathematician. I can't balance a checkbook. He is methodical, highly organized. I live under a deluge of unfiled paper. He will shop only under threat of divorce, or worse. I consider the local mall "retail therapy." His idea of a nature walk is a round of golf—in a cart. My idea of heaven is an all-day hike in the Grand Tetons. But in fact we do share a basic value system, a philosophy about personal responsibility and the importance of character. And there are other shared tastes: a love of music and history, an addiction to newspapers and current events, a passion for sports. Neither of us has much leisure time, but when we do, we watch baseball, listen to Mozart, or play tennis. Or work! Because for both of us, digging into a challenge on the job is actually relaxing, often more fun than typical leisure activities. It's not that we are "workaholics," it's simply that we find great joy in what we do.

How do we balance all of this? While we both face tough deadlines, my husband's challenges are a lot more important, and more complicated. Solutions to these complex problems are usually not self-evident. As a result, he needs a good deal of quiet time at home, to read and think and write. He studies data intensively before making decisions. One other occupational hazard—crises are hardly predictable, often interrupting scheduled vacations and family holidays.

Although we are interested in each other's work, there is a great deal that we cannot discuss. Much of what he does is highly confidential, or even classified. He doesn't talk about his work at home, ever. And he never betrays any sign of stress. It can be a bit unsettling to hear on television or the newswire that he has made a major decision, and realize that I had not even a clue that he was working on something important.

What many people who watch his somewhat arcane speeches or congressional testimonies would never expect is that he is also very funny. In fact, he makes me laugh much of the time. And despite his many responsibilities, he does not take himself seriously. That's one of his most endearing qualities. All things considered, we are pretty lucky to have found each other. Especially since I can't imagine anyone else putting up with either of us. **Andrea Mitchell**

Ruth Asawa Artist
Architect Albert Lanier

My father came from Japan to the United States in 1902 and my mother in 1919. I was born in 1926. There were seven of us and we grew up on my parents' truck farm, growing vegetables until World War II when we were sent to an internment camp in Arkansas. Father went to an Asian camp in New Mexico, so we were separated. I graduated from high school in camp. The living conditions were terrible, but our life before that wasn't much better.

A lot of people became bitter about their internment experience. I had a wonderful English teacher, Mrs. Beasley, who said it was a terrible thing, but I had to go on with my life. She urged me to go to college. I went to Milwaukee State Teachers College because the tuition was only twenty-five dollars a semester. When I left camp all I had was train fare to Milwaukee.

After Teachers College, I went to Black Mountain College and studied there with wonderful people. At Black Mountain, people were frank and open. Being a contributing member of the community was as important as your formal studies. Everyone had to wash dishes, haul coal, and work on the farm, faculty and students alike. It was a small, isolated college that accepted black students, which was unheard of in the South at that time. I met my husband, Albert, there in 1947. His sense of humor appealed to me. Albert had a very good sense of humor, an acid kind of humor.

Interracial marriage was a very risky thing to consider. California repealed its law prohibiting it only nine months before we were married in July of 1949.

Albert and I don't interfere with each other professionally, but he supports my work. Although we have never had a lot of money, we have given our time to our community. Our common interests are probably gardening and children. If Albert and I could spend a whole day together, we'd probably weed. We don't golf. We don't ski. I can't swim. I can't ride a bike or skate. I can't do any of these things. I like to weed and grow vegetables, draw, and sculpt. Arts and education were and are important now. We are right there. Our family is right here.

Ruth Asawa

When I met Ruth, she was the most exotic thing I had ever laid eyes on, not that I'd laid eyes on so many. I was enamored of her and the work she was doing. We did not have dates, we worked together. She agreed to marry me, but she wanted one more year at Black Mountain. We wanted the impersonal and diverse nature of a city. San Francisco was a new frontier for us. Neither of us had a degree. We thought we could make a living by our wits, and we did.

Our children are our best friends. Today many people wait until they can give their children all the things they didn't have. We believe that they would rather have what we already had. Although Ruth's childhood was hard, it had a marvelous aspect—working with her parents, brothers, and sisters growing things.

Shared interests help make our marriage work; shared interests and having something to talk about, other than paying the bills or the mortgage. We are always working on projects together, with the kids, and now with our grandchildren.

Albert Lanier

Alexandra Schlesinger Housewife

Writer Arthur Schlesinger, Jr.

Marriage remains the ultimate mystery. What is it that attracts people to each other? What is the chemistry of love? Why do some marriages work and others collapse? What sustains affection through long years? What explains the curious phenomenon by which two thornily independent people fall into a state of mutual dependence? No outsider can pronounce on the inwardness of a marriage. All couples are odd couples. Every marriage is a mystery, even to the participants.

Some forty-five years ago I was crossing Harvard Square on a November morning and suddenly caught sight of a glorious-looking young woman, tall, erect, blonde, beautiful, evidently a Radcliffe student. I paused for a moment in silent admiration; then went on about my business. A few weeks later in New York, shortly before Christmas, friends with whom I was having dinner took me to a cocktail party. As I entered the room, I saw, framed by a window overlooking a street on the Upper East Side, the same glorious young woman.

This time, taking advantage of cocktail party camaraderie, I approached her, introduced myself, and discovered that I knew her mother, the painter Lily Cushing Emmet. Alexandra, who was indeed a Radcliffe student, was on her way to spend Christmas with her mother in New Orleans. I found her shy, intelligent, graceful, filled with charm, spirit, and reserve.

Back in Cambridge, my wife and I invited her to the parties we occasionally gave for the Harvard and Radcliffe sons and daughters of friends. Alexandra invited us to dances at boathouses along the Charles. After college, she disappeared to Europe. In the early 1960s she returned to New York. She was now working for the *New York Review of Books*. I was in the Kennedy White House. On occasional visits to New York I took care to see her. Then I was saddened and indeed chagrined to learn that she was about to be married.

In 1966 I moved to New York. My marriage was disintegrating; so, I soon understood, was hers. We began seeing each other, then decided to live together. For a time she resisted the idea of marriage. "I was married once," she said, "and didn't like it." Eventually she relented.

I recognized how blessed I was to spend the rest of my life with this splendid young woman, nineteen years younger, six inches taller, an adored mother and stepmother, and a spirited, stimulating, refreshing, invigorating, talented, and tolerant (most of the time) wife. The years pass, and we do not bore each other. Alexandra, my love, is my fountain of youth.

Arthur Schlesinger, Jr.

Philip Johnson Architect

Freelance Curator David Whitney

I was born in a typical Puritan, New England–conscience sort of a place in Cleveland in 1906. My father was a prominent lawyer there, a farm boy who'd moved to the city and got big. I was brought up to try to be like him and of course failed miserably. I was always gay, but I didn't know it. I was attracted to different boys at different times; boys older than I in school and younger than I when I became older. It seemed a perfectly natural development to me. I didn't suffer from it, I didn't think about it until much later when I went to Harvard to study philosophy with Whitehead. Then I had a nervous breakdown, that's what they called it in those days. I took a year off from Harvard, and then later another year because I was so mixed up in my life. The neurologist said my homosexual struggle was a difficult one and the cause of my troubles. I wept most of the day and had violent mood swings that drove my family up the wall, but at least they did receive me at home.

David has been a mainstay of my life since 1960. I was quite ill recently. Everybody gave me up but David. He told the doctors I was going to be all right and I am. I am not as steady and steadfast as David is. I'm more brilliant. I know more about books. He doesn't read. I'm more intellectual. What good is that? He's more straightforward and clear and caring. He takes the lead a good deal. It's a wonderful feeling. It's hard to imagine life alone. It's a very happy life. David likes it when he can suggest something in such a way that I think it's my own suggestion. He's very smart in handling people, which I'm not.

I don't see anything different in a homosexual and a heterosexual relationship. What life is easy? Life is no good. Ministers used to tell you, "You'll get over that, young man. These are passing fancies when you're young. You'll be all right." Soothing syrup. That settled me in Christianity right away!

What makes our relationship work is a mutual respect and friendship. When we disagree, we know it, let it pass, and get back to things we agree on. I don't think my relationship with David has changed over the years. In a sense it's changed because it's less physical. As the years go by, you're not as passionate, as physically in love. You become more accommodating and at home. It's very satisfying. I think he likes me because I'm a good recipient for his theories on art. I like him because he likes me. **Philip Johnson**

Philip was giving a lecture at Brown when I met him. We were talking and I asked if I could come down and see the Glass house sometime and I did. We are extraordinarily lucky that we've been so terribly happy for this long. We've had a couple of fights that lasted a day. That's remarkable, especially because neither one of us is particularly weak.

Normally, I don't think a relationship can last as long as ours has. I've loved every minute of it. People usually have disagreements or they're not interested in the same things. It's pure luck. We've been together for thirty-nine years. We have things in common and I think we love each other, but I'm not sure I believe in love—I never have known.

I'm a very difficult person, but I haven't eaten Philip alive because he's strong enough that it works. There are so many things he's not interested in because all he's interested in is architecture. I have a broader spectrum. I'll make decisions about our daily life. It could look like I was pushing him around, but in fact he wants to be pushed around.

You have to be comfortable with each other. Sometimes you have marriages where there's social climbing at work. That's not the case with this. There's no game. I like everything about Philip. Einstein once said, "My wife takes care of all the little things and I take care of all the big things." I think I take care of all the little things. **David Whitney**

Ellis Marsalis Musician and Teacher
Homemaker Dolores Marsalis

When I saw my wife for the first time, I thought she was a real cute chick. I was hanging out on the beach with a couple of friends. I spoke to her in the vernacular of the day. At first, I didn't always act the way one should act when getting to know somebody who is really special. It was a while before I realized the quality of person she was. When I did, I thought that she was too good for me, that I wasn't the kind of person she needed to have.

It took a long time for me to appreciate the support I was getting from Dolores for my music. There were two kinds of musicians: the ones trying to get some hits, and the crazy ones like us who were really trying to create some music. We practiced in the house all day and night and we had no idea what the end would be. When I was with Al Hirt's band on the road, I came back with a trumpet for my son Wynton and my son Branford had a clarinet that I had used. I'd go in the living room and we'd have jam sessions. The jam sessions were like . . . whatever you hear, then you play that. I'd try and trick 'em and run some things in different directions. I never could trick Branford. I don't care what I did, he could always hear where it was coming from.

There were a lot of lean years, but in many ways, we were never "poor" in the negative sense of poor. New Orleans was fertile ground for jobs with music, even though they didn't pay a lot. We didn't have a lot of expenses because we didn't have habits. Dolores had a home economics degree, so we always ate very well. She knew where the vitamins and minerals were. I didn't get what the lady across the street called "a real job" until 1974 when I began teaching.

I married Dolores because I felt she could make something out of me. It was selfish, but for me, at the time, it seemed like the right thing to do. It was. **Ellis Marsalis**

I was seventeen years old, just out of high school when I met my husband. I didn't really want a deep understanding of him at first. It was very frivolous. Eventually, we got together. I admired him for his musical ability and then we went through a lot of situations that made him my soulmate.

The first time I really felt special in my life was when Ellis asked me to go on a gig with him. I said I couldn't do it because it was a white club down on Bourbon Street. He told me I was going to go, and that I was going to sit right in the front. I said, "I don't know." Ellis said, "Well, I know!" We went to the club and I sat in the front and was served. I felt so special because blacks always had to sit in the back of everything, and we usually weren't allowed to go in white clubs at all. It really did impress me. He was wild. I admired his wildness. It attracted me so.

I was born in New Orleans and we were impoverished, but my family had spiritual values that I respect and love until this day. I can remember my aunt always saying at the dinner table, "You should never steal. You should never lie." Those things stuck with me. I participated in everything, all the church and school ceremonies. I helped in the community and became a very active person.

I had high ambitions for my children. We were never able to do anything outside the black community, so I wanted them to have the opportunities we didn't have. I had a very smooth, very structured operation at home. All the kids practiced their instruments for half an hour a day before dinner. Then after dinner, they did their homework, and after that they could watch television.

Ellis is a very knowledgeable man and very kind, but complex. There are times I don't understand him. We've been married for forty years. I got married for keeps. I've learned a lot of lessons. We're not just the "happy couple." We've been through it all—good and bad, happy and sad. It makes life real and it makes me real. **Dolores Marsalis**

Martha Parker Hall Artist

Artist John Hughes Hall

I simply can't talk about marriage. It's too difficult, both the talking and marriage. I've been married three times, leaving two husbands. To my great surprise and delight somewhere along the line I became a painter and a collagist, and a wife, again. I have been married forty years to my present husband! The pluses in marriage are certainly far greater than the minuses. I have no advice to give anyone about anything.

Martha Parker Hall

I was born in New York City in 1913, attended private schools in New York City and New England, and graduated from Princeton in 1935. I've worked as an architectural designer, journalist, and artist. I've lived on Cape Cod longer than in New York, married four times, the last time for forty years. I stopped drinking alcohol forty years ago. Perhaps there is a connection.

John Hughes Hall

North Bennington, Vermont 1995

Allen Shawn Composer

Writer Jamaica Kincaid

for Jamaica

VALENTINE

Moderato ♩=ca.100

Allen Shawn

Maria Cambareri Retired Seamstress
Retired Factory Worker Luigi Cambareri

My husband will be ninety in August and I am eighty-three years old. We met in the Italian countryside, in a town named Solano Superiore. It was an arranged marriage by my father. Luigi and I are second cousins.

In Italy during the war, it was horrible. They used to give us a quarter pound of bread for two people. If we fed our kids, we couldn't have bread ourselves that day. We also made bread, but we had to hide it. If you bought a pound of meat, you had to hide it. We had to move out of the house my father built for me until the war was over. That was the war.

We wanted to come to America because there was nothing in Italy. There was no living. For us it would have been all right, but for the children, there was nothing over there. Here it is different. You go to work and get your money. You can buy a house. You can do anything. We gave the house here to one of our sons. We have to do what we can for each other. Now we live with him and his family. At a certain age, if you don't have anything, it's better.

A husband and wife have to be good to each other. We never fight, thank God, never. He is always quiet. I cook every day at noon for Luigi. You have to wash the clothes, clean the rooms. I always do whatever I can in the kitchen, every place. I love to wash clothes, hang them, fold clothes, do everything. I like being married. Otherwise I'd be alone. What could you do in this world alone?   **Maria Cambareri**

I liked the kind of family Maria grew up in and I liked the way she kept herself. She was very neat and quiet. She was a good lady and she was a good worker. She was going crazy for me and I went crazy for her!

When I saw her the first time, I knew that I wanted to marry her because she was beautiful. A lot of women wanted me, but I told them to keep quiet because I already found who I wanted to be with. Some people choose their wives from a photograph. You can just tell; there's a certain quality and you can pick them out.

I came to America for my sons, to give them an opportunity. I would be living a more relaxed lifestyle in Italy. When I came to America, I went to school to become a United States citizen. I've never used the English language again. I live in an Italian community, worked with Italian people, and I always speak Italian.

Maria and I have always been happy together and have always managed to work everything out. Now that we've gotten older, we're still happy, and still working out little things!

Translated from Italian.   **Luigi Cambareri**

James Lovell Veterinarian and Retired Missionary
Preacher Francine Lovell

I wasn't born-again when I married my first wife. She prayed for me for eight years until I accepted the Lord. Things were said and done that hurt my wife and brought her to tears. That creates a cloud over a marriage. It's like the tears of Jesus. I could see that my selfish behavior was causing unhappiness to my wife. When I made the decision to accept the Lord, it made a big difference in our marriage.

When my first wife died, it was a devastating experience for me. We had been married for thirty-seven years and I was lost without her. During that time following, I lived near the Endtime Handmaidens. I planted a big garden and worked in it to raise vegetables for them down there. I'd go home in the evening and read the Bible. I could see that life is very fragile, like a vapor, here today and gone tomorrow. What time I had left in my life, I wanted to spend serving the Lord. I asked the Lord to send me a partner who loved the Lord and wanted to serve the Lord.

My marriage to Francine has been perfect. Since we've both been married before, we never let any disagreement develop into a serious problem. It says in the Bible, do not give place to the devil. A good marriage is made of love, trust, honesty, and communication. If people don't have that trust, they lose communication, and it breaks down the relationship. If you both love the Lord more than you love each other, it's going to be a strong marriage. It says in the Bible that a threefold cord is not easily broken. When you just have two it doesn't make a good rope.   **James Lovell**

I am French. This part of Arkansas belonged to France. The word Ozark was never written O-Z-A-R-K. It was written A-U-X space A-R-C-S. It means, "Where you see the rainbows." And I think the word "Arkansas," pronounced as it is, was taken from the French, A-R-C en C-I-E-L, which also means "arc in the sky." I feel I have come home.

On the sixth of October 1982, I received what I believe was a word from the Lord. I read in the Bible, "And thou shalt be called by a new name." God told me I was going to be married again. I was divorced and had lived alone for twenty years. God started to show me rainbows. Everywhere I went, I saw a rainbow; in a shop window or in cloth or on somebody's purse. One day, I saw an arc on a brochure, an invitation to a convention of missionaries in St. Louis. I was being called. Jim, my husband to be, whom I did not know, went to the platform after I gave my word and said he was a candidate to the marriage supper of the lamb. In my heart I heard differently. I heard him say that he was a candidate for marriage. God opened my heart to tell me that Jim was the one I was going to marry. If you have been renewed in spirit and if your heart is opened, then those things work magically.

Jim and I met a week later in Arkansas where the organization who'd held the convention was based. I opened the door, and Jim walked in. He lived next door. We started to break French beans together and I began to feel pure love for him. We met again in Israel a few months later and it was on a walk on the shores of Lake Galilee that Jim asked me to marry him. In the last ten years, we have traveled together to sixty different nations, going to preach the word of God. Two years ago we stopped traveling so much.

Jim and I have a radio program that preaches over the belt of Africa. Through it we speak to about a hundred and sixty million people each week in their dialect. They gather around short-wave radios to hear our program.

The name written on the front of our house is "The Ark." Jim placed it there when he built the house, long before I came here. He thought of Noah's ark and he thought of Arkansas. Praise the Lord!   **Francine Lovell**

Shirley Eason Assistant Principal

Mail Carrier Henry Stanton Eason

The first six years of marriage are the hardest. It's a transition time. It doesn't mean you give up your total identity, but it does mean there are compromises you have to make. Stan and I were both free-spirited. I loved to go with the girls, taking trips and going shopping whenever we felt like it. When you get married, you're held accountable for what you do.

As women, we are the ones with the most patience. It can be an advantage to cementing a marriage. Men have always had their moms. We're like surrogate moms but on different levels. What you have to do when you marry someone is be very patient with them and love them enough to understand their mistakes. Mothers tend to enable sons to be who they are. We want to do the same for them. Women have always said they do eighty percent more work than a man does. We always will. We always have. That's just the way it is. I think it's because the Lord knows that we have more strength than men do.

There are times when things are not smooth with us. We've had our arguments. I believe in legal pads. We each write down what we can't stand about the other and then we switch off and look at the other's list. Then we switch back and circle the five things we *really* can't stand. We try to change and alleviate those things. You have to work at it. You're going to always make mistakes, but if you really care for each other, and you really love each other, you will try to work it out.

Shirley Eason

My great-grandmother Lucinda Bland lived to be 107 years old. Lucinda used to smoke a corncob pipe and drink a little moonshine every night before she went to bed. Television frightened her. Gunfire from movies scared her. She had lived through some of the hell-raising in the country area. Her great-grandmother was one of the first slaves to come to Georgia, to Johnson County. I was born in 1946 and the only boy. I wasn't spoiled because we were a little too poor to be spoiled. We didn't realize we were poor because everybody else around us was a little poor.

I was a confirmed bachelor, but my wife, Shirley, came to a Christmas party I had and I've been hooked ever since. I had to get to her before the sharks, my buddies, did. We got to talking and she was different from anyone else I knew. She carried herself differently. She didn't chase behind me. She was independent. The hook was in my mouth and I was trying to spit it out. I didn't want to get married. I was a little afraid but finally gave in. I'm still in love with her. The spark is still there. At times, I send her flowers, just on the spur of the moment. We've been married for twenty-three years, have two children, and just had our first grandchild.

I love walking and I've been carrying mail for over twenty years. I could ride, but you don't get to meet the people when you're riding. You do a whole lot of lookout for your customers. With the crime rate, a lot of the older people are afraid of opening their doors. Even if I don't have any mail for them, I'll knock on their door anyway and wait for them to holler back. I want to make sure they're OK. It makes them feel better to know someone cares. You've got to have respect for the older people. They've earned their way and one day I hope some young guy will be looking out for us.

Henry Stanton Eason

Fifi Pate Housewife

Publisher Lynn Luckow

In college I met the man I married; we were each other's best friend and shared the same philosophy. We had forty-eight years of a wonderful marriage but no children. He came home when I was thirty-seven years old and said statistics proved I would be a widow, and probably for many years, so I should be thinking about what I wanted to do.

I decided to study art. I began going to the great retrospective exhibits from Chicago to New York, and then to the library. In those thirty-four years, I got a very good art background.

It was about three years after Charlie died that I began wishing I could meet some nice man, fall in love, but not get married. Two years later, I was visiting one of my gay "sons" in San Francisco and met Lynn. We were instant friends, and since he came to New York often we became very close. We have a great relationship. We travel a lot, usually with art leading us to certain places. We have both become collectors and share the same philosophy of life. We believe strongly in supporting charities and in kindness in general. It could not be a finer friendship; in our years together we have had no disagreements. May I live to be at least one hundred years old in this great joy of living!

Fifi Pate

It was love at first sight. A dessert party capping a memorable black-tie evening, and Fifi was the only sweet of interest to me. The room was crowded and I sat at her feet in my tuxedo, and we talked endlessly, barely stopping to take a breath. She was the first Fifi I had ever met, and soon I realized there was but one Fifi in the world. It was August 20, 1988, and I was in the presence of a Princess.

As we parted I asked if she would consider dinner the next time I was in New York City. A nod of consent said yes, though she was quick to add that her calendar was filled months in advance. Within a week I phoned and our first date was set for Café des Artistes.

From our first dinner together and the day at the Metropolitan Museum of Art that followed, our fate was sealed. We discovered common values, an appreciation for art, the importance of truth, a passion for cassoulet and most anything French, a sense of mutual admiration and respect, and an uncommon love for both urban and rural life and for each other.

In our first decade together, we shared gourmet meals in restaurants of renown and ate pitchfork fondue in Medora, North Dakota; we drove the coastal highway from Northern California to Vancouver, and crossed the continental divide by train in a thunderstorm; we experienced the holidays in bustling London, and found solitude in the season in Santa Fe; we attended the San Francisco Opera's premiere of *War and Peace* and celebrated Zubin Mehta at his farewell performance with the New York Philharmonic; we laughed, we read, we talked, we corresponded, and we enjoyed quietude.

We engaged each other and life with the joy and heartfelt enthusiasm of new lovers. No subject was taboo and no secrets were hidden from view. Our relationship was clear. The Princess and her Viking had fallen in love. Indeed, in everyone's eyes, including our own, we were a couple.

Lynn Luckow

Shirley Hamblin Chain Saw Repair Shop Owner and Operator

Oiler for Duke City Saw Mill # Wayne Hamblin

I met my husband when I was in seventh grade and he was in ninth. I fell in love with him right away, but he didn't know I existed. After we graduated from school, we ran into each other while we were Christmas shopping with our mothers. We were both bored to death. That's when we started dating, Christmas of 1966. We were married in March of 1968, and have been that way ever since.

We're very close and sit many hours holding hands. We're not much on words. We just look each other in the eyes and know what the other is thinking and feeling. We don't talk about those kinds of things much.

Wayne was raised Mormon and I joined the Church after we were married. His family has been in the Church since it was started in the 1800s. The Church is geared toward family life, strong ties, and building moral strength in the family. We believe families will be together forever and we try to live by the standards Jesus has set.

We taught our children how to work. All our children know how to cook and clean and sew and can, our three boys and our girl. Our girl knows how to repair chain saws and automobiles or toasters or whatever breaks down. We taught our children to be self-sufficient. **Shirley Hamblin**

Shirley is the only person in the world that is right for me. She's been a good friend and a good companion, a good partner. She's been everything I could want in a wife. We haven't had any trouble getting along with each other for thirty years. She's always been somebody I could talk to, been there for advice and counsel. We tried to make decisions together.

We're both able to work from sunrise to sundown. Shirley's one of those very few people in the world who can do anything she puts her mind to. We got the kids all through college, debt free. They've all got good jobs and they're all married. We just had our third grandchild and the family's still growing. We've been lucky.

We've moved back up to Colorado now. We've got thirty-five acres and we're out here on the hill, just Shirley and I and the dog. The stars are so bright, and the wind blows in the trees. We've got a big flock of wild turkeys; five or six deer that stay here most of the summer; the elk we see when they're passing through, when they come out of the high country in the winter and when they go back in the spring. We've had two bear come visit us; that was kind of fun. We get away from the TV and the phone and all that stuff that makes noise. We've got a big old long porch on the backside of the trailer and we sit out there in the evenings and listen to the quiet.

We've slowed down a bit. The world's moving too fast. Other people can chase it. We've got as much of it as we want.

Wayne Hamblin

Ronald Gault Investment Banker

Journalist Charlayne Hunter-Gault

Almost thirty years ago, Charlayne and I met in Washington, D.C. We were both busy pursuing our respective careers, and our lives somehow were very full even before we became an item. She was a divorcée in progress and I was single, smart, self-confident, presentable, articulate, etc. You get the picture. Early in the relationship, Charlayne invited me to dinner at her apartment. Candlelight, mood music, a romantic setting. I had brought a bottle of wine. It did not stop there. She had cooked a wonderful meal and for dessert, there was a deep-dish pie with a wonderful flaky crust. It was topped off with ice cream. It was a fabulous meal and evening. I ate all of the food, including two servings of that dessert, and drank all of the wine with very little help from Charlayne. Stimulating conversation about her work and mine, a lot of touching, hugs, kisses, and tenderness. It was not long before we starting seeing one another regularly and I looked forward to those very special dinners for two. Armed with her black pot and skillet, Charlayne had beaten off fairly intense competition. I was too stuffed after those dinners to visit any of my usual haunts, hang out with my buddies, or conduct any solo prowls.

Perhaps, the most important thing in our marriage is that we have tried to make it fun, even though we consider ourselves serious people and approach our commitment seriously. Love, friendship, mutual respect, thoughtfulness, and sensitivity are important ingredients in a marriage that works. Thirty years and two kids later and we seem to have it about right. But there is always that next challenge: aging parents, children chasing their own dreams, finding enough time to live life to its fullest, and keeping all our traumas in perspective. A friend said once, "This ain't no dress rehearsal." He wasn't talking about our marriage but I often think he could have been.

Ronald Gault

It was not love at first sight. Maybe it had something to do with the place where we met: the Washington, D.C., morgue. We were both covering a controversial police killing of a black civilian during the turbulent late '60s—I for a local television station, he for the Justice Department, where he worked. Or maybe it had something to do with a new acquaintance who had earlier insisted that I meet a guy named Ron Gault because she could just feel that we were "made for each other." My skepticism bordered on outright rejection owing to the fact that she was a young graduate of an Ivy League school, white, and though sweet and smart and endearing in her bubbly enthusiasm, didn't strike me as someone who would understand what kind of man would be right for me. In fact, the image I conjured up in my mind was of a "proper Negro" of the Ivy League kind. A "Hi Guy" kind of guy. Thanks, but no thanks.

But the second time we met, the "proper Negro" turned out to be a man of a most different kind. I had been looking into a story that someone told me Ron Gault knew a lot about. So I phoned him and he invited me for lunch at a popular soul food restaurant. In those days, most brothers (and sisters) usually dined heartily on pork chops, or chitlins, collard greens, potato salad, and cornbread, or some equally cholesterol-filled fare. I was struck when my lunch companion ordered a discreet bowl of gumbo and a glass of white wine. HMMMM, I thought, as I took a closer look. And lo and behold, I really liked what I saw, from the natty suit and tie, to the '60s afro and beard, to the insightful intellect with all kinds of good information about the story I was pursuing and more. And "pursue" became the operative word in both our cases. And not just the story.

Fast-forward three years. We are lying on the deck of a boat in Long Island Sound. As a warm sun caresses us as we caress each other and a gentle wave rocks our boat . . . OK! . . . I'll finally admit it: I propose. And from that weekend adventure to the Rock of Gibraltar where we were married shortly after, to the top of Aspen Mountain and down—maybe before I was ready, but not daring not to meet my husband's challenge—there and many other places—high and low, in the world and in my head and heart. I have been challenged by and in turn challenged this very different kind of man—to love with a love that is "more than love," if not at first sight, at least for all time.

Charlayne Hunter-Gault

Tony Randall <small>Actor</small>

<small>Housewife</small> Heather Randall

I had my first child at the age of seventy-seven. I was married for fifty-four years and my wife and I just couldn't have children. We tried to adopt and that didn't work out. At the age of seventy-seven I found out what most men find out in their twenties. If I were a poet, I could possibly put it into words, but I'm not. It's a joy, happiness, revelation, a source of such deep pleasure and wonderment, the wonderment of life and watching it develop. My daughter's reached the age now where there's some response, you get something back, and oh my! All my life, I felt that's the only thing I've missed, because I've had a marvelous life, a wonderful career, and a wonderful, long marriage. I always thought I'd had everything, but I gave up on having children. I thought that was the one thing I wouldn't find out about. But now, that's come.

I don't worry about Heather. She's a survivor. She's the best companion possible: funny, a wonderful cook, and born to be a mother. She was a good actress and she probably will be an actress again. She's a very able person: smart, driven, ambitious. She knows what she wants and she goes for it. She has energy and a plan. I choose to believe her when she says she loves me. There are girls who love older men, who want older men, and I'm lucky that I found one. **Tony Randall**

I am twenty-seven years old. I don't feel an age difference between Tony and me. We have a lot in common. We both love theater and the arts. Believe it or not, he's got this very suave edge, but he's like a little boy sometimes. He's happy to jump around and make jokes. He's always joking.

The first day I met Tony, I didn't like him. But when I got to know him really well, I thought he was a wonderful person. We were friends for several years. After his wife died, we became closer. I graduated from college, and so I was out in the world alone and he was widowed. I liked older men, but not that old! I never thought we'd be together, but you just don't know with love what's going to happen. It's unpredictable.

It's morbid to think about the fact that most of my life will be spent without Tony. He talks about it a lot. He probably wants me to be prepared. I try not to think about it too much because it's depressing, but it is a fact of my life. However long we're together, it's worth it. **Heather Randall**

Maxine Hong Kingston Writer

Actor Earll Kingston

Earll and I met in college. We were both English majors. We have the same education and the same intellectual discipline, which is a strong bond between us. We've been married for thirty-three years.

I liked the expression on Earll's face when I first met him—his eyes and his mouth. He had a very amazing smile. And the way he looked at me—an open and kind expression on his face. He was also verbally expressive, and so funny.

Education and our arts give us a lot in common. That's probably one of the things that makes our marriage work, but it's deeper than that. It has to do with our essential natures, our souls, our very basic psyches. We have a definite predisposition for each other; the way we were raised and grew up as children somehow matched as we got older. There is a largeness in Earll's being that could match whatever I needed to develop in myself. As we went along during these decades, we could keep finding each other along the road. It's almost like meeting again and again and again.

Maxine Hong Kingston

Max's roommate and my best friend were dating, and Max and I tagged along as a double date. They eventually broke up but we stayed together. We got married in 1962, so we were kind of post-beatnik and pre-hippie. We all used to write and read our things to each other in those days. I think Max was the only woman reader among all these guys. It was a little bit awkward, because we were all writing one kind of thing, and she was writing something else.

On our first date we went rock climbing at Baker Beach near the Golden Gate Bridge. Max was really feisty. I looked at her fearlessly climbing up those rocks and I admired that. She was cute as hell, too, cute and funny. She was very smart. I really liked her family. I was an only child, so it was a terrific thing to become a member of her big family, although it was sticky. I didn't find out until twenty years after we were married that her mother still called me "the boyfriend." I never really did learn Chinese. I'd rather not know what she was saying about me!

Max still surprises me. She sees things. That's wonderful. I think we are getting to the age when we are beginning to develop something like a collective or joint memory. Max will fill in what I forget. I love her very much. She's a terrific person and I feel myself lucky to be along for the ride with her.

Earll Kingston

Lobsang Lhalungpa Buddhist Scholar
Editorial Assistant Gisela Minke

Until his early teens, Lobsang—a monk in Lhasa, Tibet, and son of the former chief State Oracle—had never set eyes on a Western person. When, in the 1940s, he met Colonel Tolstoy and Captain Dolan, special emissaries to Tibet of the United States' President Roosevelt, he was amazed.

Gigi had never set eyes on an American until 1945 when, fleeing from East Germany with her family, she witnessed the arrival of American troops near Hanover. As the first United States tanks rolled in, all manned by African-American soldiers, she too was amazed.

Nothing would have surprised them more, in those years, than to have been told that one day they would be married to one another, living as United States citizens in Santa Fe, city of American Indian, Spanish, and "Anglo" cultures.

Before they married, in 1980, Lobsang had toured Germany as a guest of the German government; Gigi had made eleven trips through the Himalayas and had spent many winters in Tibetan refugee camps in India, where her two Tibetan foster children were living.

They say it is good for an intercultural marriage to be on neutral ground. Santa Fe, with its different cultures and cosmopolitan flair, is the perfect place for Gigi and Lobsang to live—on a mountain overlooking the wide open spaces of the American Southwest. Lobsang feels this landscape resembles the highlands of his beloved Tibet.   **Gisela Minke**

Woody Vasulka Video Artist

Video Artist Steina Vasulka

The first thing Woody said when we were introduced was, "Hey, get me out of this place! Marry me!" "No problem," I said. "Let us do it!" At that time marriage was almost the only means for Czech citizens to leave the country.

I used to ride around Prague on my moped. That seemed to upset the Czech male population a bit. "A woman on a motorcycle! Would she be able to start it?" They would stop and watch. Unfortunately, the moped was a lemon and sometimes indeed, it would not start. So when Woody offered to fix it, it seemed only reasonable that I, in turn, would get him a passport.

I would find him panhandling outside the dorm where he would keep begging until he had enough for a classy dinner in a fancy restaurant. With Woody's expertise of the best restaurants in Prague and my valuable foreign currency, we entered into our first great collaboration, and in no time I became poor.

Getting a marriage license was complicated. The Communist regime had no use for international love affairs, and sent us to the Ministry of Foreign Affairs. When we finally received the reply, it said that the Czechoslovak Socialist Republic would consent, provided that the Republic of Iceland would give its permission in writing. My father explained to me that since Icelanders could marry anybody they wished, nobody had any authority to issue such paper. "I don't care, just do it," I said. So one late night after a few drinks, he and a colleague in the State Department broke into the presidential office down the hall (there were no locks on the doors), and wrote on the presidential stationery in a florid longhand of ancient Icelandic, that the Icelandic nation descending from a long line of noble Vikings had no objections to this affair. On this parchment paper they then melted red wax and sealed it with the presidential seal.

In January of 1964, in the medieval City Hall of Prague, Woody and I signed the contract.　　**Steina Vasulka**

Sherry Kern Registered Nurse

Float Designer and Artist Blaine Kern

I find Blaine so incredibly interesting. I'm not interesting like he is. The age difference doesn't bother me. Blaine has so much energy. He's attractive. He looks good. Everybody loves him. He's a local hometown hero. He's been tremendously successful, so for me it's like a Cinderella story.

In New Orleans, we have some of the best food in the world. Blaine and I have a lot of fun going out to eat. He says all the women he's known in the past ate like birds; he says I eat like a bird, but more like a vulture. My plastic surgeon loves me!

Blaine's in the limelight and I enjoy that because I'm in his shadow. Even when you're in his shadow, you still get a little bit of attention. My job is being a good wife. I know my role. A lot of it is to support Blaine, to keep him rested, fulfill sexual needs, make sure his tummy's full, keep him in shape. Last year was Blaine's fiftieth year in business. He's like Peter Pan. He never ages.

If I'd known how wonderful being married was, I would have gotten married a long time ago. I was thirty-one when we got married. Blaine is thirty-six years older than I am. You see that a lot in the South, so nobody pays much attention to it.

Blaine had been a bachelor for almost twenty years. There have been a lot of adjustments. We have to work at it. Those who say they have a perfect marriage are lying or in denial or have a poor memory.

I work at my relationship all the time. We have to work at it every day. It's not easy, but anything worthwhile is never easy. I read books on the psychology of relationships and on sexual techniques. Blaine and I go to Catholic Mass every Sunday; we're both very spiritual, which helps.

Sherry Kern

I'm a ninth-generation Algerine and my eleventh-generation grandson lives across the street from me. I remember working on the riverfront with my daddy, painting signs on tugboats and barges and ships. As a child, I read H. G. Wells and Arthur Conan Doyle and Jules Verne . . . I was going to the moon! You've got to dream of something before you can build it. I've built a Mardi Gras empire.

I've originated and reintroduced double-deck and triple-deck floats; when I first came to work, the floats were built on old Spanish-American War caissons that held only eight or ten people. Now I've got floats holding 130 people. I started animation on floats. I introduced celebrities to Mardi Gras; brought in Danny Kaye, Jackie Gleason, Bob Hope. Mardi Gras is a billion-dollar-a-year, taxable industry. The city of New Orleans gets forty or fifty million dollars a year from Mardi Gras; it pays for the police, the firemen, all the sanitation. If you make New Orleans a queen, and that queen has a crown, the most beautiful gem in her crown is Mardi Gras.

I met Sherry at a Mardi Gras ball. I saw this beautiful young girl. She was dancing with somebody else and I cut in. That was it! She called me afterwards. I didn't remember her name, but she sent me a bottle of sherry to remind me who she was. She came down here and we had a seven-hour lunch. We were married a couple of years later.

Sherry is extremely intelligent. She beats me at Scrabble all the time. She's vivacious, loves people, and of course she's very beautiful. She's an incredible cook and loves to do the yard work. She does things you'd think a man would do. Our yard is the prettiest yard in Algiers.

It's great having such a young wife. Sherry is a tremendous hostess with all the balls and parties that go along with the more than thirty parades a year I do in New Orleans alone. Everyone likes her. I didn't think I'd ever marry again but Sherry's a nurse, so I figured at my age, I need a nurse. That's a joke!

Blaine Kern

Millie Card Retired Beautician

Dairy Farmer Earl Card

I love Earl so much I could eat him up. I've always lived on the mountain, and when Earl and I were courting, he would ride through a blizzard on horseback to see me. Earl is very good-hearted and good-natured. All the women kiss him, but I can still trust him, thank goodness!

Earl's helpful in every way. He's a good baker and a good cook. He never complains about anything. He's very handy. As a matter of fact, he did all the washing today. We go to the lines when it's sunny. I remember when I used to go out there, I'd put Earl's hip boots on to go hang up the clothes; clothes would freeze before I got them on the lines and I'd freeze too. Now I've got the dryer down in the basement, so we're very lucky.

We had a scare recently. I wanted to call 911, but Earl told me to call our daughter. She took him over to the emergency room. I was scared. I should get used to it because he's had so many of these heart attacks. He was on oxygen all the time. He had pneumonia and bronchitis, too. He never tells me how he feels. All I have to do is look at him. **Millie Card**

I've tried to be good to Mommy because she deserves it. We've been through a lot together. We've both tried to pull our weight. There were rough times, but I always wanted Mommy to stay home and take care of my kids.

I used to get up about twenty minutes to four, do what I had to do, milk the cows and so forth. I'd come in, take a quick clean-up, have a cup of coffee, and head to work. I worked for forty years at a state school for the mentally ill. I got through at two o'clock, came home, changed my clothes, and farmed until ten at night. I always made fifteen hundred bales of hay every year. I boarded horses, sometimes twenty-five horses or more, had some cattle and hogs.

After we built the barn, just before we started making hay in June, we cleaned the barn out and had a square dance.

We even put in a little blacktop so we could have some more square sets outside. Over the years I think our biggest form of recreation was square dancing. It's a lot of fun and we made a lot of friends.

You've got to have something to live for along with your family. I would be lost without some animals around. I have about thirty chickens. They're getting old: I didn't get any new ones this year. We have Charlie the dog, and Bonnie and Clyde, our cats. Since the donkey is gone, Perky the horse, who's thirty years old, has decided I'm his buddy. When he sees me he starts snickering, and when I get down to the gate, he has to kiss me all down this side and that. The old fool!

The thing that makes Mommy the happiest is doing something for someone else. As long as she could, she'd help anyone out. I'm devoted to her. Since she first broke her hip, she's been laid up half the time. I've taken over the housekeeping. It's not as good as it would be if she was doing it, but it's worked out very well.

We've been married fifty-three years. We all have our little quirks and whatnot, but Mommy and I just overlook them. We've usually agreed on how to raise our kids and when we had different ideas, we'd talk about it. We've never had any arguments, big arguments at least. We don't ever go to bed at night mad at each other. If there's disagreements, why, we get it settled. **Earl Card**

Rettakudi Nagarajan Certified Public Accountant

Kolam Maker Pichammal Nagarajan

I accepted a Hindu arranged marriage with Picha when I was twenty-two, which meant no dating and accepting my father's decision. Even though love started slowly after marriage, it hid for a long time behind my desire for asceticism, control, career, education, and male supremacy. Over the past forty-four years of married life, and after many ups and downs, love solidified. It was a result of a deep sense of commitment, monogamy, religious duty to be faithful to her, and a realization of her great and sincere contribution to me and the family. Of course, Picha had to demand such attention and love, and is still waiting to see their visible proof!

I didn't realize it when I came to America in 1966, at the age of thirty-seven, that I would find it so difficult to accept the decisions taken by my children, which conflict with our views of the Hindu family values. I am very much interested in religion, politics, and social service. My life's mission led me to participate in the building of a magnificent Sri Siva Vishnu Temple, a beautiful temple and a place of traditional worship for thousands of Hindus in the Washington area. It was built by the community with the devotion and prayers of hundreds of volunteers, donations of millions of dollars, and beautiful work of artisans from India. God gave me and Picha an opportunity to be a small part of this grand endeavor and devote our best efforts in community service.

Rettakudi Nagarajan

The drawings at my feet in the photograph are made by my hand every day. They're called *kolam* and made of rice-flour. They are drawn by millions of women in Tamil Nadu on the thresholds of houses and temples. It is a popular Hindu practice in the state of Tamil Nadu in southeastern India where I come from. When my husband and I first came to America, we were in an apartment, so I could not put the *kolam* on the threshold of the house. The gods were not that important to me, back then. I just carried on with life. I got inspired by a visit to my home village, Kunnam, in 1979. In the house where my mother had once lived, I wanted to make the *kolam*. Good things started coming when I made the *kolam* more and more.

My husband was the fourth or fifth man that I saw when I was a young girl. In every household, the *mamiyar* (mother-in-law) was *sadhu* (gentle). My brother met Rettakudi's father on the railways. Both were seated near each other and they began talking to each other. After some time, each realized that they had a possible match.

We were all so impressed that Rettakudi worked at the telephone office. For me, it was like a spaceship would be to you. My brother talked to Rettakudi's best friend about his qualities and my brother was told he was a really good man. My brother asked, "His lips looked black. Does he smoke cigarettes?" We noticed that he was a little plump. But everyone said, "Picha will get a little plump, too, so that is OK." Everyone said, "He is really messy. She keeps everything neat." We were well matched!

I got interested in marriage when I saw a film in which there was a wedding. I started to desire a husband. The arranged-marriage idea was important to me. "I cannot always stay at my brother's," I thought. I got married. That was how life was. We live well today. That is what I have come to now.

Pichammal Nagarajan

This interview with Mrs. Pichammal Nagarajan took place in the fall of 1998 in Tamil, and was conducted and translated by her daughter, Dr. Vijaya Nagarajan, theologian and anthropologist.

Norman Mailer Writer

Writer and Painter Norris Church Mailer

I look at this photograph as if I did not know these two people but am intrigued enough to study them. She seems so strong, so beautiful, so centered. She is in command. He hovers in the background. He is much older than she is, and his jacket does not fit; he is overweight; his pants will soon be very wrinkled.

Yet these two people are together. There is something odd about their relationship. They should not be in the same frame, yet very much they are.

The answer is clear to me, but then I need only step out of the fiction that I do not know them. Of a certainty, I understand why they are together. They have a hundred relations with each other and here there is only one. Since she used to be a fashion model, she likes being photographed; she is comfortable before a lens. He hates it. He is much too vain to have to consider his flaws now that the camera is no longer his friend.

Still, they do have those one hundred separate relations with one another and it keeps them powerfully together. They have been with each other for twenty-one years and have not lost interest. If a strand wears out, there is always another, then another. Soon there will be one hundred and one relations. He could even adore the idea that they share a romance if only they did not have to take pictures together.

Norman Mailer

I am twenty-six. Divorced for two years. A high school art teacher in Arkansas. I am ready for an Adventure.

He is a walking Adventure. Fifty-two. Dangerously attractive. Masses of salt and pepper curls. Clear blue eyes. Married five times, seven children. A reputation as a brawler. Womanizer. Genius. What girl could resist?

We meet. Walk out onto a porch hanging over a brook in the woods of Arkansas. He tells me in full eloquent paragraphs how attractive I am. My eyes. My nose. My mouth. The rest.

"You certainly know how to deliver a good line, Mr. Mailer."

"It's no line."

"I don't care. I have always bought a good line, well presented."

The Adventure begins. I take my first plane trip. New York. Restaurants. Shows. Jazz. Friends. The subway. Romance.

Time to leave.

"Don't go back to Arkansas," he says. "Stay in New York."

I consider for two seconds. Tops.

"All right."

I quit my job. Pack up my three-year-old son, and move in. I am twenty-six and a half. I can take care of myself. If this mad romance fizzles, I will move on. Live each day as it comes. Enjoy the Adventure while it lasts.

A few years go by. We have a son together. Get married. Seven children have become nine.

Nine extraordinary individuals.

One man.

My life.

Twenty-one years have passed. He was telling the truth.

It was no line.

Norris Church Mailer

Evelyn Lauder Senior Corporate Vice President

Chairman and CEO Leonard Lauder

Just as the United States was entering the Second World War and after having fled Vienna, my parents brought me to New York City. This was my mother's dream come true.

Because I know what we left behind in Austria at that time, I truly understand the meaning of freedom and how beautiful life is here in America.

Leonard and I met on a blind date, arranged by a friend, when I was a freshman in college and he had just entered Officers Candidate School in the U.S. Navy. I guess this was, although I didn't realize it at the time, a life-changing moment. We were best friends for about three years and I didn't think he was really interested in me. Suddenly, however, our friendship developed into something else, like a blossom suddenly opening on a bare branch. We married in 1959, have two gorgeous sons and daughters-in-law, and now there are four unbelievable grandchildren.

The life we lead is an example of what everyone can accomplish in this country if you want it badly enough. Combine that with good health and very good luck, and you have nothing about which to complain. **Evelyn Lauder**

Although both of my grandparents were born in Europe, both of my parents were born in the United States. And even though I'm only second generation, I feel very, very attached to America, attached in more ways than I can describe. I got my education in New York City public schools, and later on at the University of Pennsylvania. The most important event in my life and in my love of America was going into the United States Navy. Being in the navy gave me a sense of this nation and a sense of its power and the great people that make it up. The only thing I regret is that we don't have required military service today. I think every young man and woman should do some sort of national service so they can understand the greatness of this nation.

I met my wife-to-be when I was in the service. I would show up at her doorstep, and we'd see each other for a bit, and then I'd leave again, and show up again several months later. During that period of time, my regard for her grew enormously. I saw what a genuine person she was and how interesting she was to me. We got married in July of 1959, ruined everybody's Fourth of July weekend, and it's been the most incredible relationship ever since. We each married our best friend and we remain each other's best friend.

Leonard Lauder

Ayana Karanja Assistant Professor and Administrator

Community Builder and Organizer Sokoni Karanja

I grew up three miles south of where we live now. My mother was a dressmaker and my father was a tool and die maker. Everyone was black in our community except the shop owners. Blacks grew up on the south or west side. Sokoni and I met at a research institute called the Adlai Stevenson Institute for International Affairs. It was housed in Frank Lloyd Wright's Robie House at the University of Chicago. I was a program coordinator, and he came in as a Fellow.

I thought Sokoni was a nice man. I felt very comfortable with him as if he were someone I had always known. We had a very pleasant, interesting, and fun kind of romance. We got married about a year later.

It was after the civil rights movement that we met, and there was a consciousness about Africa and a romanticized notion of what Africa is. It is important for African Americans and blacks from other parts of the diaspora to go into Africa, to the reality. It is a different experience than can be easily explained, and one all black people ought to have for the sense of place it provides. Sokoni and I had a lot in common in the way we viewed the world and what we thought African Americans ought to do and needed to do in order to create a stronger community. Education is very important to both of us. Politically we were very much aligned and had a lot of energy to work for social change for all of our people. That was very important to us then, and continues to be.

The secret to making a marriage work is not ever feeling that it has worked, but always recognizing that it is a work in progress. You must always give it primary attention, lest it slip away. Hopefully, you change every day. Your consciousness changes. You change physically, psychologically, and politically. You change in every way if you are a thoughtful, introspective individual. And so if you have two people, two spheres, as it were, two consciousnesses moving in different directions there has to be something that pulls you toward the center, and you have to work very, very diligently to make sure that that core remains in place. There are many things to pull you away, and there is really nothing to hold you where you are except your desire to be there. **Ayana Karanja**

I was an athlete, so I didn't pay tuition, but I had to help take care of my family, because by the time I was in college, my father was deceased. I worked at a boy's industrial school in Topeka, Kansas, at night while I went to Washburn University. That's where I first learned that what I could really do well was to work with people. I began to realize that I needed to understand families, how communities work, and how people live in communities.

I pursued my education and got three master's degrees (in experimental psychology, social work, and urban planning). I went on to receive a doctorate in urban planning and economics. Ayana and I worked together to begin the organization I work for now, called Centers for New Horizons. We started it in 1971. It still exists and it's bigger and more difficult than ever. The focus is to revitalize the south side of Chicago; to help families develop in such a way that they can contribute to the revitalization of this community. We have an African-centered approach, in that we believe that people have to have an appreciation of themselves in order to really go outside themselves and address the building of family, building of community, building of anything. You first have to build and understand yourself before you can go beyond yourself.

In a marriage, each person has to be willing to do a hundred percent even if you are only supposed to be doing fifty percent. You have to be willing to extend beyond that middle ground because some days the other person may not be able. One of us has to pick up the pieces and make things work for that particular day. As long as you care and communicate during those moments, when one is not quite able, the other always manages to move across the divide. **Sokoni Karanja**

Maggie Kirn Writer

Writer Walter Kirn

We got married when I was nineteen and we've been married for three years. The age difference of fourteen years was scandalous when we got engaged. It threw people for a loop.

I like being married to Walter. We're really good friends and it's nice to have your best friend around all the time. There's nothing wrong with growing up with someone. You don't necessarily have to be grown up when you get married. After all, when are you grown up? If you get married young, you understand the ultimate truth that we never are who we are.

Everyone said Walter would be a parent to me, but I haven't found that to be true. Quite the opposite! We almost have a sibling kind of relationship. There are very few differences between the two of us when we're alone together.

Maggie Kirn

Maggie and I are probably the unwisest match ever made if you go by conventional wisdom. I can't imagine two people from more different backgrounds. Maggie grew up living the high life in Hollywood and I grew up on a little farm in Minnesota. When she showed up in Livingston at age eighteen, she had a wild experimental college haircut and wore baby-doll dresses and go-go boots. She was a ball of fire and a real shock in this town. I was intimidated but incredibly drawn in at the same time. I was scared, thought I might not be up to it. I couldn't imagine being more attracted to her, nor could I imagine getting into any more trouble with anyone.

I came to Maggie with preconceptions and she turned out to be the most down-to-earth, fresh, and loving person I'd ever met. It was a real quandary for me because it was the first time in my life when my heart and my head were absolutely at odds. My head told me this was, on paper, the worst match ever made. My heart told me that I loved being with her. I'd made a best friend and she was gorgeous. I'd grown up with high feminism in the '70s and '80s, so Maggie's desire to get married and have a baby was startling. She insisted she wanted to be a teen bride. I've never been so glad for doing a crazy thing and I've never been so comfortable having done something that others felt unwise.

I'm amazed that someone with Maggie's background has been able to stick it out on a ranch in the middle of nowhere, and has become a leader in a community like this. This relationship started out as almost illicit. I thought I was making the pornographic and not the practical choice, and then it turned out to be both. That doesn't happen very often. Nobody told me it could. You don't pick your love and your mate. She's picked for you and you either run away or you let it happen.

Walter Kirn

Jacob A. Arlow <small>Psychoanalyst</small>
<small>Housewife</small> Alice Arlow

While I was distantly aware of Alice in high school, when we met again two years later, I fell madly in love with her, and told her I was going to marry her. She was not impressed. In background and temperament we were quite different. She was quiet and reserved. I was not. She already had a boyfriend who I felt was wrong for her and, in classic fashion, I set out to rescue her. It took two years before I won her over.

While our temperaments and interests differed, our goals and values were the same. Both of us were deeply affected by the Holocaust, so we were determined to have a large family. And to fulfill our unspoken aspirations for the American dream, we decided that we would live outside the city. So, although earlier we had considered ourselves members of the avant-garde, eventually the pattern of our lives turned out to be quite conventional.

Living in what was a small town in 1946 posed a number of problems. My professional orientation was metropolitan, not suburban, so that meant I had to spend long hours in the city, and not participate as much as I would have liked in the raising of our children. In retrospect, I feel that my professional success could never compensate for the time lost from the family.

In old age, husband and wife get closer with each succeeding year. Consideration for one's partner, compromise, and a good sense of humor become important. For the most part, it was Alice who indulged me in my interests, specifically my passion for travel. Clinging to the tall grass on the slopes of an extinct volcano on Easter Island, Alice looked over to me and said, "You know, I have just been asking myself, 'What am I doing here?'"

"I recall for you, the affection of your youth,
The love of your espousals.
How you walked after me in the wilderness
in a land that was not sown."
Jeremiah 2:1–3

Jacob A. Arlow

Although we really met at the age of eighteen in a Hebrew-speaking camp, I had a vague memory of Yakie (that's the Hebrew nickname for Jack) from high school in a third-term French class: an eager know-it-all, with his hand raised all the time, wanting to give the right answer. I was not favorably impressed. He seemed to think he knew all the answers to everything and didn't hesitate to say so. Usually, however, he was right.

Our birthdays are only seventeen days apart. When we were eighteen, we started seeing each other consistently and married six years later. We have now been married sixty-one years. My opinion of him continues to change over the years. Now I feel he is great and keeps on getting better. He is a lot of fun and a source of endless knowledge. I am always very much interested in hearing what he has to say, both in the sphere of psychoanalysis, of which I know very little, and in many other things as well.

If I were to give advice to young people about how to make a marriage work, it would be: patience, tolerance, compromise. Marriages don't always start happily. They work themselves out in time. It all depends on what the goals are and what people expect. In our day marriages were expected to last a long time and compromise was the way of working things out. Most of the compromises, it seems, were effected by the woman. It is all very different nowadays.

It's always a good thing to be in love. It helps. With us, it exists.

Alice Arlow

Larry Schaaf Art Historian
Archivist Elizabeth Schaaf

My upbringing was overwhelmingly normal in small-town Illinois, with an exalted sense of the present, no idea of the past, and a constantly looming burden of the future. One's job defined one's being. At the university (Illinois, of course) I discovered photojournalism. I hated engineering and finally succeeded in flunking out of it. Lots then changed. I joined VISTA and was sent to the first foreign country I ever visited— Houston, Texas. That eventually led me to Austin where I serendipitously discovered the history of photography. The future and the present shifted to the past.

When I moved to Baltimore, it was on a quest for a doctoral degree. In my spare time, I followed my usual pattern of hunting down leads. It was in the pursuit of a portrait of George Peabody that I met Elizabeth. In an otherwise stormy period of my life (and I know it sounds trite), she was a burst of sunshine. I've since found out there is a full range of weather available in there, but Elizabeth usually manages to find something good or something humorous or at least something ironic in virtually everything. She is self-sufficient and she is tremendously creative. It shows in what she says and it shows in what she does. We broke up for the last time when I left to work at the George Eastman House, and we were married in a magical fifty-dollar potluck wedding the following New Year's Eve. Friends from all strands of our lives somehow got together and made it work. We honeymooned in Crystal City, Colorado, in a marvelous nineteenth-century hotel an engineering friend was helping to restore. We were the only occupants and woke up to the sound of hammers and electric saws (the workmen had kindly tarped off a bridal suite for us).

No two years of our marriage have been the same. Elizabeth has made me realize that I can be an independent researcher and still consider myself to be a real person.

Larry Schaaf

I grew up in Maryland on a farm that had been a present to my grandparents from my great-grandfather. We actually had one of those mythical extended families that included my mother's brother, my wonderfully eccentric Aunt Sarah, my brother, parents, and grandparents. My marriage to Larry was not my first (we don't all get it right the first time). I was divorced and very happy with my life when I met Larry. I enjoyed my work. I had a good horse and a wonderful borzoi named Lubov. My children were off but living nearby.

On a day when I hadn't time to even stop for a cup of coffee, I'd been given advance warning that some dreary art historian was headed my way to inquire about the provenance of an unremarkable portrait of George Peabody. Well, in walked this gorgeous creature wanting information on what turned out to be a dinosaur from the dawn of photography by Mayall. Tracking it down is another story but, miraculously, I found the documents he needed. I decided to drop off the photocopies since he lived only three blocks from my house.

I was about to leave a note in his mailbox when his roommate appeared. The three of us ended up having oyster soup and afterward Larry and I went out for a long walk. It was a beautiful October night and there was a full moon. I'm not sure it was love at first sight—but it was amazing.

We've been married—is it sixteen years? I can't imagine what it would be like if we weren't interested or involved in one another's professional lives, since both of us are so absorbed by what we do—especially Larry, who spends most of his waking hours amid his books and files. Our dogs and my young Arab, Magic Minstrel, get me out to the country on a regular basis. Larry thinks fresh air is unhealthy.

Larry is always full of surprises. One summer, he decided to put a pond in our back garden. The pond was Larry's excuse for not doing our kitchen. It's a small, oddly shaped pond, with goldfish and a little brown garden rat who lives under the waterfall. She uses the water hyacinths for boats (as well as salads). She jumps onto them and glides out to the center to gather up fish food. I feed the fish and the little garden rat comes out and waits until she can catch a ferry.

Larry's work involves a lot of travel. When my own schedule allows, I travel with him. We've shared tables in libraries, each involved in our own projects, sharing discoveries and musing over problems together. It all works and happily so.

Elizabeth Schaaf

Shawnna Conrad Child Care Provider
Carpenter Slate Boykin

I first met Slate when we were nine years old. He and my brother hit it off right away. They are both the type of boy that makes your mother cringe, the tree-climbing type of boy. Slate started coming to stay with us, sometimes three or four days out of the week, sometimes two weeks, three weeks at a time. During the summer he practically lived there. His mother would have to threaten him and drag him home. I thought he was a brat. He would torment me and I used to hate him.

I was pretty rowdy, keeping up with my brother, whom I worshiped. He was the bravest, strongest guy, and Slate was very much the same. Slate is fearless still. It's hard for people to believe Slate's so gentle, because he's quiet and big; you can't always tell what he's thinking. He doesn't have a violent bone in his body. He appreciates things that a lot of people take for granted or overlook: the quiet, the solitude of being in the woods.

In some ways, we have a traditional Karuk Indian life. The men hunt and fish and the women take care of it once the men get it home. Slate built me a smokehouse so we could do all our smoking. We make traditional meals. We gather acorns, grind them up, and make acorn meal. Slate loves doing all that; he's grown up with it in our community. He never takes me away from my culture. In the Karuk world, the place where we live is the center of the world. Everything starts here. There are dances, religious rituals, ways of being that are all part of our life. It is something Slate is comfortable with and we're raising our children that way also.

Slate has always been familiar to me and that is something that is special about our relationship. There is so much I don't have to explain to him and there is so much he doesn't take for granted. **Shawnna Conrad**

I get real frustrated living in society, all balled up with anger. I'm not such a social creature, so it helps living out in the woods. Out here I accept who I am.

My mom fell in love with some crazy hippie guy, and that's how we wound up in Forks of Salmon when I was a kid. I became best friends with Shawnna's brother; we both loved fishing. We had a wild time on the river for a long time.

When Shawnna and I were kids, we didn't get along at all. In a couple of instances, she'd throw rocks at me, even come at me with a knife once in a while. She knew I was allergic to cats and once when I was sleeping out in the trailer, Shawnna snuck in with a cat and threw it in my sleeping bag. By the time I woke up, I had a huge asthma attack, but Shawnna got a kick out of it! We didn't see each other much for a long time.

We both went off to school, but I didn't like college, so I came back home and started enjoying the river life again. Shawnna came back, too, and we got an eye for each other. It wasn't real serious at first or I didn't think it was. Then our son came along and changed all that.

We're still not married, but we'll probably get married in the future because Shawnna wants to. Shawnna is strong-minded and really powerful. She's kind of a medicine woman. She stands her ground real well. I don't know how she puts up with me, but she does. It's a pretty balanced relationship. Sometimes she wears the pants a little more than I do, but I kind of need that. We joke a lot together, which keeps us on our toes and helps us get along. **Slate Boykin**

George Plimpton Writer and Editor
Homemaker Sarah Dudley Plimpton

I met Sarah at the Los Angeles Olympics in 1984—odd that I had not met her before. For many years we had lived two doors away from each other on a Manhattan street. I would like to say that in Los Angeles I met her when she tumbled into my arms after winning the 100-meter high-hurdles, panting heavily. But it wasn't anything like that at all. She had been brought out from New York to organize entertainment for corporate clients and I had been engaged as a featured speaker. We found time to go to some of the track events and, of course, the closing ceremonies which featured fireworks, of which I am inordinately fond. We discovered we had much in common—friends, backgrounds, likes and dislikes. I think one finds that it is hard to imagine oneself without such-and-such a person—a kind of wondrous acceptance that this is how things should be.

George Plimpton

When George and I were married, I joined a rather large extended family composed of his Yankee relatives and various athletes, poets, writers, dreamers, and adventurers of all sorts. He has an almost limitless capacity for friendship and enthusiasm for life which he shares generously with me. If this all seems rather ethereal, I will tell you that what I love most about him is his magnificent head of hair—it drives me wild.

Sarah Dudley Plimpton

Bernardine Dohrn Child Advocate
Professor of Education William Ayers

Bill and I met in June of 1967, a week after I graduated from law school and had moved to New York. We met in Ann Arbor at a conference called "Radicals in the Professions." It was the week of the Newark riots and it was a real jumping-off moment, not just in each of our lives but in the country's life. We danced all night and we were friends for five years. The falling in love came with that long cushion of friendship and common ground.

By the time we fell in love, we were living underground. We were part of a community, an outlaw culture. We were in opposition to the way things were—to the Vietnam War and to racism in particular. There were moments that were scary and full of high drama, but it was mainly ordinary.

Just as we had our two babies, the underground shifted and the political organization (the Weather Underground) and the swirl of the anti-war movement we were part of ended. We became a couple in a different context, with little kids. Our life for the last twenty years has revolved around them.

We still think we're radical organizers. Our works have had the thread of children, of working with children and for children. It's a fabric and definitely a world we didn't imagine would be in the late '90s; a society that in many ways hates kids, has turned against its own children and demonizes kids. Who could have imagined that? For me, the big blessing is a shared vision and a lot of laughing. **Bernardine Dohrn**

When Bernardine and I fell in love, we were in our twenties and we were busy building a revolution. Both of us were drawn to and active in the most militant displays of opposition to the Vietnam War. In 1970, a house in Greenwich Village blew up and three of our close friends and associates were killed. We were indicted on federal conspiracy charges and we decided not to show up in court for the scheduled court dates. For eleven years, we were on the run. Bernardine was on the "Ten Most Wanted" list for several years, a personal vendetta of J. Edgar Hoover's. We had seen many, many good people who were opposed to the war, who were involved in civil rights and black liberation movements, spend an inordinate amount of time defending themselves. That then becomes its own logic. Instead of spending time building a movement, or opposing the war, you spend time with lawyers figuring out how to defend yourself against a conspiracy indictment. We decided we weren't going to do that.

It was 1981 when we turned ourselves in. The conditions had changed and the reason for our going on the run had gone away. Bernardine was put on probation. The federal indictments had been dropped against us. Under Watergate and the Freedom of Information Act, the illegal activity of the government surfaced. Now it's hard for people to remember a time when the government was trusted. Before that, it was assumed that if the government indicted you, you were guilty. We were indicted and we weren't guilty; in fact their methods for gathering those indictments were themselves illegal.

Our children were born underground. For us, these two boys that we had, and the third boy we adopted, have become not only the center of our lives, but in many ways, the embodiment of our hopes, too.

We met in the turmoil of the social movements of the '60s, and part of our falling in love and our relationship ever since has been entwined with the quest we were both on individually and then together. In some sense it continues to this day—a quest for a more decent, just, and peaceful world and a saner social order. It's not just that our intimacy was born in that moment, but our intimacy continues to find meaning in that goal. We're at the point in our lives when we finish each other's sentences. **William Ayers**

Willem Malten Entrepreneur and Buddhist
Painter Marion Malten

Since the beginning of Marion's pregnancy, everything has been colored by the prospect of bringing new life into this aging world. I had been thinking about the portrait session and suggested to Marion the possibility of doing a nude photograph in the now luscious garden. So, we walked out of the house at about six in the evening, sun softening, through a primitive arched gate into the garden, passing the blooming gladiolas, marigolds, cosmos, and nasturtiums, picking and chewing lemon basil, while admiring the ripening tomatoes. I took my clothing off shamelessly, while admiring Marion's protruding belly, and her full tits and her rounded hips. So there we were, not just nude, but naked, under two giant sunflowers bent over by the weight of their blooms.

Yesterday, my wife and I drove out to the Santo Domingo Pueblo, south of Santa Fe, a far distance from the native Holland of my childhood. We went to see their biggest tribal dance of the year. Imagine! One thousand dancers of all ages; men, women, and children all doing the footbeat to the rhythm of just one drum, beaten by an old man sunk into a trance. In the midst of the pink dust cloud that the stamping feet kicked up, I suddenly realized that one group of painted men, who were moving ever so gently but ecstatically in between the rows of all the other dancers, were impersonating the beloved spirit of Blue Corn. On top of their white-painted bodies with black dots all over, on the top of their heads, they had tied corn husks, like feathers, pointing at the sky, attracting a heavy black rain cloud ready to unload its contents onto our heads—the promise of rain, the semen blessing of the father sky coming down to fertilize the mother earth. This recognition was very moving to me and I know why. It was a taste of the delight in fertility that must have been prevalent for all archaic humankind. It is proof that there must have been a time when knowledge meant intimacy, the seemingly forgotten gateway to understanding.

Willem Malten

Willie Gordon Attorney

Writer Isabel Allende

When Isabel and I met, I had been a bachelor for almost seven years, and I was very gun-shy about relationships since I, at least, hadn't found much desire for mutual reciprocity in the ones that I had fallen into and out of during that period. She was different. The first thing she asked about was commitment. She also said something to me that I have shared with many other couples since then: she told me that she would never do anything to intentionally hurt me. I believed her and hence entered into one of the most amazing experiences of my life, for the time we have been together is truly magical. I had been waiting for Isabel for fifty years.

Yes, we have suffered unbearable pain together, but we have also had many wonderful experiences with family and friends all over the world. I would say that the reason we click so well is because our energies combined multiply in amazing ways. Together we seem invincible. The result is something to behold.

Willie Gordon

Willie and I met late in life, when we both knew who we were and what we wanted from a relationship. We were not willing to settle for less. We were looking for absolute love and we had the good fortune to find each other. So many things have happened since we met several years ago that we feel bound together forever. We have had happiness and adventure, but also terrible pain, like the death of our daughters Paula and Jennifer. All that has brought us very close; we hold each other in a profoundly spiritual way.

Our greatest pride is our little mixed family, which grows in spite of the losses and the obvious differences between all of us. I think that the essence of our marriage is mutual sympathy, which makes us tolerant of each other's defects and mistakes. I really like Willie, and our time together is precious to me. We share almost everything, but we also respect each other's space. Intimacy and trust are the other pillars of our marriage. And, I have to admit, eroticism, which only gets better as time goes by. I hope that we will always want each other, that we will sleep entangled in a tight embrace to the last day of our lives . . .

Isabel Allende

Paris Swoopes Retired Custom Tailor

Retired School Teacher Reba Swoopes

My mother's father was white and her mother was part Indian. In those days, the Afro-American woman had no control even though she was a freed slave. They were just turned loose as animals and had to survive as best they could. The white man did whatever he wanted to. My grandmother was just sixteen years old and never did particularly care for my mother because she resented the way my mother was conceived.

I was born in 1902. My father had the barbershop downtown in Sheffield. I finished twelfth grade, having to go from town to town to do it because Sheffield only had school for blacks through the seventh grade. After high school, I went to the Tuskegee Institute. I returned to Sheffield and went into business in a hotel. A friend of mine ran a pressing shop down in the basement, and he let me develop my tailoring skills in his shop.

A white friend of mine asked me to make him a suit, serge blue. His friends saw it and after a while, the basement shop was too small. So I borrowed fifty dollars from the Sheffield National Bank, loaded my personal belongings on a horse and wagon, and drove down to Second Street where I opened my own tailor shop. I was able to bargain for a building on the main street.

Sheffield has changed much for the better since I was a child, but it is no utopia. There was a time that we couldn't think about going to a restaurant and sitting down to eat; we had to go down to the back by the swill cans and have a little setup back there. If you went to a doctor, you couldn't be serviced until after hours. I'm not bitter. They thought they were right. I respect myself and others respect me because of it. Everyone in this town respects me, black and white.

I was married to my first wife, Mary Swoopes, for fifty-two years. She and I got along fine. We had three children; one's still living. Reba and I met about six months before we got married. We were compatible. She is a compassionate person, very intelligent, and she and I like to travel. She is interested in people and so am I. The only contrast is I am a member of the Baptist Church and she is a member of the Church of Christ Faith. We have an understanding. You remain that and I remain this. Don't try to make me that and I won't try to make you this. It has worked so far. Got my fingers crossed! It's imperative to have a home, not just a house. You can see a beautiful house, but it's like cats and dogs in that house; it's not a home. As of now, we have a home. **Paris Swoopes**

My first marriage wasn't good. He was a cheater, so I let him go free. Then I married my second husband, a wonderful marriage until the day he died. I won't find anything else to beat it. We had harmony, no arguments, nothing.

I'd only seen Paris one time before his son-in-law introduced us. That was when I had lost weight and he took the pants up for me. When I really met him I thought he was wonderful. He was lovable. He was just the type of man that you would appreciate. There's an age between us. I'm eighty and he will be ninety-four. It makes a difference. I didn't ask him how old he was until after we got married.

To make a marriage work, be fair, and have no secrets. Learn to like things, or compromise. That's what you have to do, not have the whole thing one-sided. My religion is very important to me. Everything is there in the Bible, and all you've got to do is read and apply it to everyday life. That's what makes life sweet. We don't have music in my church, but we sing. I sing when I cook, too. It makes days move.

Reba Swoopes

Jennifer Steele Businesswoman
Writer Edward Bunker

This year marks our twentieth anniversary, and in rereading his love letters from twenty years ago, I don't think (at 26 years old) I stood a chance of resisting him. I was twenty-three years old when I first met Eddie. I had an unbelievable curiosity about the world he had come from, the adventures he had experienced. He had big dreams, painted on a large canvas, spoke of fire and brimstone. I had a deep belief in a power of redemption, and the symbolic significance of the Prodigal Son.

When we first met, I was his counselor. I immediately expressed interest in reading his first novel, *Straight Time,* and he immediately brought me a copy with the inscription: "To Pretty Jennifer, my counselor, who will school who?" In fact, we both have schooled each other. He may have needed me more desperately for his very survival and staying power, but I needed him equally for my fulfillment.

Our romance did not begin until a few years later. We lived in Brooklyn Heights at the toe of Hart Crane's beloved Brooklyn Bridge—one of my favorite poems in high school. New York was a new adventure and Eddie opened up a world to me. We met other writers, artists, and intellectuals with whom we discussed books, ideas, politics, history. This was a world that I had never seen before but one that I found wonderful. He gave me all that, and I gave him an emotional conscience. He had lived outside the law, but within his own world he had a high code of ethics in terms of personal loyalty and not hurting people weaker than himself. My background was loving, with a strong religious and spiritual foundation. My secure family background was the wellspring to taking such a risk on love. I never underestimated the power of love. Love has transformed him—slowly and over twenty years—and of course I am not the same person either.

Jennifer Steele

Life does not change swiftly. It changes like a ship; you've got to change it slow. The idea of redemption in America is very rare. Once you're locked up you're locked out.

If ever in reality a relationship personified the myth of Beauty and the Beast or the attraction of opposites, it is my wife and myself. Her parents celebrate fifty years of marriage; mine divorced acrimoniously when I was four. She went to riding school; I went to reform school. She graduated from the University of Southern California. I graduated from San Quentin. She was a sorority girl. I was among the Ten Most Wanted. We met when I was paroled to a halfway house following my third term. I was forty-one, she was twenty-three, and the epitome of the California girl: tall, slender, blonde, fresh as a rose, and younger than springtime. She'd even read a book or two, and some of my essays in *The Nation,* so they made her my counselor. There was no romance. She was married, so there was no more to be said. Even if she hadn't been, I had no idea what my life would be, so I left the halfway house and California altogether, but we kept in touch and remained friends.

Two years later (I'd never gone a year without at least an arrest), things were different. I had published a second novel, written a screenplay and, at least for the moment, was in a truce with the world. Plus she was now divorced, which made possible the exploration of a relationship. In my wildest fantasies I never imagined it lasting longer than a year or so. We were unimaginably different, as much as yin and yang. On previous occasions, women who had gotten close to me were hurt by unintended "collateral" damage from my ongoing war with the world. I vowed that, however long it lasted, that would not happen here, so that whenever it ended, she would look back and say the memories were good. If it lasted two days or two weeks, I hoped to make it worthwhile for her. It has been two decades. Not only is she more than ever the love of my life, ours is a tale from which myths are made, as special as Quasimodo and Esmeralda, who lie together under Paris.

Edward Bunker

Phil Peterson Harley-Davidson Dealer

Housewife and Church Activist Charlotte Peterson

I grew up on a cherry farm in Door County, Wisconsin. One day a bus pulls in with eight girls in it between twelve and fourteen years old. I picked out one, my Charlie here. She was twelve years old and I was fourteen. She was my dream-type girl, my fantasy. We kept up the friendship. We couldn't date— her mother wouldn't let her date until she was fourteen. By then I had a car. We went roller skating and to fairs. We corresponded when I was in the navy and she was in college. After the navy, I went to the University of Wisconsin to wait for Charlie to graduate. I was there to play football and wrestle, but I got kicked off the football team right off the bat for riding my motorcycle on the practice field.

As soon as she graduated, I quit school. We got married at Christmastime 1947, fifty years ago. I married my dream.

It's unusual for somebody to have an idea of playing football and having a motorcycle, flying a plane—a lot of people have those fantasies and they don't actually do them. I've done it. Most people don't because they listen to their wife! She never did stop me from doing anything.

Phil Peterson

As children our summer job was to pick cherries. It was fun because we were with all our friends, and of course Phil's family owned the orchard, so he was there being a boss, hauling the cherries into the factory. I was fourteen when I had my first date with him. We went roller skating. Every summer we would get together and spend time together.

Phil always loved motorcycles, but his father hated them. His father didn't allow him to have one or even talk to the people who had one. When he came out of the service, the very first thing he did was buy a motorcycle. We would ride together because my father was a motorcycle enthusiast. When I was a little kid, my father would take us to all the races. Phil started racing and he'd always run into Harley Company people at the races. When he was quite young and before we actually got into the business, one of the owners said to him, "Why don't you quit trying to kill yourself on these motorcycles and be a dealer?" He got that bug in his bonnet. The cherry business wasn't good; the crops were being frozen out and the trees were getting older and not producing as much.

We were having children and we knew we had to educate these children, so we tried the motorcycle business. All of the dealers in the Harley network are family people, people who have been in the business, taken over from their fathers, and we have all kind of grown up together. When we get together with them it's like a big family reunion, because there are parents and children who we have known for years. It's fun.

Charlotte Peterson

Michael Wolff <small>Musician</small>

<small>Actress</small> Polly Draper

I first saw my wife on television. I used to perform Tuesday nights at the Improv in New York. All of the performers hung out at the bar where there was a television set always tuned to ABC. At ten o'clock on Tuesdays the show *Thirty Something* was on and Polly was one of the stars. I thought she was long and tall and leggy with a sexy voice.

I first met my wife when she was a guest on a show for which I was the bandleader. I cajoled her address from the segment producer. I sent her 101 red roses, and didn't hear from her. I drove by her house and saw them lying dead on the porch. I called the florist and had some more sent every week. After three weeks, Polly called and left a message on my machine thanking me for the flowers and explaining that she had been in Canada filming a movie.

We finally went out on a date. I was heavily smitten, and instigated a period of ardent pursuit: calling often, even going over and sitting in a chair in her backyard waiting for her to come out and talk to me. I believe now this is termed stalking.

Anyway, it worked. We're now married with two sons, and living a bi-coastal life together between New York and Los Angeles, with occasional trips to Europe—wherever our work takes us. We're extremely lucky to be able to live a creative life.

Michael Wolff

I first met Michael when he was the bandleader on the *Arsenio Hall Show*. I came on the show as a guest and he hit on me in the hair and makeup trailer. I think that was appropriate because we both had extremely big hair at the time. In fact, we decided the hair must have been what attracted us to each other.

After we met, he sent me 101 roses which sadly died on my doorstep because I was out of town for a week. So when I returned he sent me 101 more and then on our first date brought me 101 more. It became a habit—he'd bring me 101 roses at the drop of a hat. I grew concerned about his extravagance. Then one day I drove him to work and saw a sign outside a flower store on his route: 101 roses, $19.99.

Polly Draper

Charles Bell Author and Teacher

Jack-of-All-Trades Diana Bell

In Mariana's photo, my smug smile may reflect the luck of a married alchemy where an in-de-god-damn-pendent TWO, over divisive liabilities, have held (like proton and electron) to the bonded dance of a functioning and transcending ONE. Though it is more likely I smile at that portrait where the painter has made me, at seventy, a lusty, 15th-century monk—described below, not by Caesar's VENI, VIDI, VICI, but by VIVI, VISI, VIBRI—I lived, I saw, I vibrated!

Charles Bell

Forty-six years of marriage. It was on board a troop ship, not yet converted back into a passenger liner, that we met. A shipboard romance that finally led to our union. To be married and remain married to a highly intelligent man with a phenomenal memory and love for literature, philosophy, art, and historic facts is a feat. I had to learn early in our life together to fight for my own identity and worth. With two very individual people, each has something to add to the other's life and they should trust in the union. For us, it worked. We laughed, we quarreled, we made up.

Most evenings, stretched out on the couch, Charles read out loud to me. We started with *Moby Dick* and worked our way through a vast list of wonderful books. Often as not, those reading sessions ended in a more physical frolic, binding us ever more closely together.

There were our walks and picnics in the woods with our children and later, alone. On these rambles I found flowers and trees I had known as a child and tried to teach Charles their names, but with little success. He did make a study of the vast and complicated oak tree family, but the others remain unnamed to him. He strides in front with great thoughts in his head; I bring up the rear tipping my hat to old plant friends.

We traveled often, either with grants or teaching exchanges, in Europe, Puerto Rico, and Mexico. We explored by bus and train the great churches and museums of those regions. We climbed mountains and wandered over large sections of Italy, Germany, and the British Isles. We picnicked against haystacks with wine and pork pies.

Although we led our lives together, we also followed our own pursuits. Mine centered around our children and relatives, on my deep love for gardening, book-binding, and writing children's stories.

Charles has taught me a great deal; my world is far richer than it would have been had we not met aboard the SS *Washington.*

Diana Bell

Santana Martinez Potter

Potter Adam Martinez

I knew Adam as a boy, but as I grew up I really didn't pay any attention to him. I grew up with my grandma and my grandpa. My grandma was nice, but mostly I liked my grandfather. He helped me in every way. He used to ask me, "Why don't you get married to Adam? He's a good man."

When Adam and I first got married, I shared a lean-to with my mother-in-law for about six years before they built our house. Adam's father and my dad helped build us an adobe and we still live in it. We used to use wood for heat but now we have natural gas, which I don't like very much. I still have my cooking wood, though.

Adam's a good man, a good worker, and he loves his children and grandchildren. We've always loved each other and talked about things, about what should be done. We both decide what's right and what is wrong. And that's how I've taught my children. So far, they're all all right.

Santana Martinez

Melanie Hope Poet and Teacher

Film/Video Maker and Writer Catherine Gund

When I first met Catherine it was a love-at-first-sight kind of thing. I thought she was incredibly beautiful. We were both part of a downtown lesbian community that liked to party a lot. I would find any excuse to go hang out at her loft which was a central meeting place in that crowd. At first we channeled our sexual energy by making a video together. That way we had an excuse to stay up until 4 A.M. without being distracted. Then of course at 4 A.M. I couldn't possibly go home so I would conveniently spend the night.

When we started out I was afraid to really let myself fall in love too fast. I felt like being a lesbian was hard enough and I was worried about getting into an interracial relationship. But I forced myself out of that fear one day when I realized I needed to talk to her every day and that if something was wrong I wanted her near me. I allowed myself to love her fully and we've been moving forward ever since. Sometimes I think we do have to put all of our eggs in one basket and dare to see what happens.

We have an amazing daughter named Sadie Rain. I want her to feel that she can make any choices she wants to about how she will live and love her life. **Melanie Hope**

One of the first things I loved about Melanie was how she talked about her childhood, how she remembered it, what she laughed about. And somehow we were always around a lot of children. I got to see her so comfortable and funny with them, easy and direct.

Melanie was the first person I'd ever met who I imagined I could be with forever. That had really never crossed my mind before, and it was such a liberating feeling. It also allowed me to begin considering starting a family with her. We took it pretty slow though and didn't move in for three years, which for lesbians is an eternity.

Having a child makes such a difference in terms of the intensity of the time you spend together as a couple and the depths you have to go. You make decisions all day long and you make them together. Shared values are important. But instead of just dealing with this as a way to parent, we also focus on it as a way to learn and know more about each other and ourselves. I'm overwhelmed by the experience in a great way.

I feel like a different person than I was before I met Melanie. One of the few linear, clear, and stable things in my life has been Melanie, spending time with her, getting to know her. It sounds predictable in a straight, traditional way: you grow up, meet someone, get married, and have children . . . but none of that was assumed in either of our lives or in lesbian lives in general. Maybe that's why it feels different. Every step has been a process of discovery and creation. I'm glad I was discovered by Melanie and I love what we create together. **Catherine Gund**

Gemma Hall Docent

Researcher Lewis Hall

Lewis and I met forty years ago. I was teaching Italian at the Berlitz School of Languages in New York where I had come about one year earlier from Italy, my native country. With the students we could only speak in Italian, so my English was not progressing very rapidly. When one of my students, an aspiring opera singer, invited me to a dinner party, I was reluctant to accept, because of my poor English. But when she mentioned that one of the guests was to be a young man who had lived in Rome for a year learning Italian, I accepted. And indeed, his Italian was very good and our common interest in the arts was an immediate bond. Lewis introduced me to the musical scene in New York and I learned a lot from him.

He was a tall young man, and when standing next to him, my small stature seemed to me even smaller! Lewis kept telling me, though, that "good things come in small packages," and that made me feel better. Forty years later we are so accustomed to each other that I don't think about it anymore, and I often even wear flats! Indeed, it is not only in stature but also in many other ways that we complement each other.

We married three years after we met and we have a daughter, Angelica, whom we also raised to love the arts. Our life continues to evolve in the same way: We still go to the opera, concerts, ballets, and museums. I now volunteer as a docent at the Metropolitan Museum of Art, where I give tours in Italian as well as in English. During all these years, Lewis has never had a chance to forget his Italian and my English has improved. It was a lucky chance that brought us together forty years ago.   **Gemma Hall**

Louis Begley Lawyer and Novelist
Writer Anka Muhlstein

My wife is marvelous. She's absolutely the best human being I know; the brightest, the straightest, the most capable of extraordinary affection, the purest. It is hard to believe she is real, but she is!

Louis Begley

My husband is extremely charming. When we were first married, there was something that always surprised me: Women stopped him in the street under the most frivolous pretext. Under the seduction and charm, he's extremely serious. Louis is a man who never gives you a glib answer to a question. When I started writing, he was the only person I could show what I was doing. I knew with complete certainty that he would tell me the truth, that he would take time to read it and think about it. It's the combination of charm and seriousness which I find extraordinarily attractive in him.

Anka Muhlstein

Leah Chase Chef

Restaurateur Dooky Chase

Dooky was a musician. Musicians are crazy as heck and the strangest thing is I liked nothing about musicians. I liked athletes because I am a buff for physical strength. He was eighteen and I was twenty-three when we met. I don't think I knew Dooky three months when we were married. We've been married fifty-two years.

My husband is totally different than I am. Sometimes, when you meet somebody and see good things about them, you like them and you get to love them. It matters little what they do or what's their way in life. My mother always told us that women truly control the behavior of men. So, if you like a person, if you love a person, then you make it work for you. If they have to play music, you understand that they have to play music. In life everything depends on how a woman handles it.

Dooky runs this business really. I do the physical work, and he keeps the books. He can keep things on an even keel. Sometimes he's too tight with the money and I have to loosen him up a little bit, but it takes two people to make things go. You can't do it by running over a person. If you have a husband and he doesn't move quite as fast as you, you have to learn when to let the reins out, when to pull them back. If you just bulldozed over the man, then you'd be living with a mouse and that's not good. You know you're going to have differences all the time, but if you truly love a person, then you get on with it.

Leah Chase

There was a physical attraction between Leah and me. I saw Leah as being the epitome of the person I thought would be best for me. She was very attractive and she was very well read and had a unique way with little children. She knew how to talk to them in a way to get responses. I saw all of that in her. I saw a complete person. She looked like the lady I wanted for my wife and to raise my children.

I had a band, so that might have been what attracted her to me, I'm not sure. I was pretty popular at the time. I met Leah at a dance when my band was playing. Right after intermission I told my band that I was going to take off a couple of songs and ask that lady to dance. I was nineteen years old when I got married.

My mother and father started the business early on in 1939. Blacks didn't go to restaurants in those days; we had what you called "little shops." My father was a very orderly man. He didn't like noise, so our bar wasn't noisy. We served sandwiches and people started to bring their families. Over time, we served more Creole food and we added an upstairs to the back of the building for club meetings and various activities. We held many meetings of magnitude addressing the quality of race relationships there. At that time in this city, it wasn't permissible for blacks and whites to meet together in public, so our private room upstairs was helpful. We had meetings with politicians, judges, and people who were meaningful in change. We solved major problems for the city. Dooky's has a history.

Dooky Chase

Lloyd Bentsen Attorney, Former Senator and Secretary of the Treasury
Volunteer B.A. Bentsen

My husband and I met at Texas University. We had six dates and got married. Cooperation, compromise, and understanding are three very necessary qualities to making a marriage work.

Lloyd is the dearest, sweetest, most thoughtful person. We don't have arguments. It's been incredible, how you can know one so little and then be so lucky. I really am fortunate.

Our life together has been the most exciting, most fabulous life. Lloyd has been in politics for thirty-two years. It's fortunate we both like people. We have met so many people all over the world. For us, it's been a wonderful life.

B.A. Bentsen

Couples leave some surprising legacies and couples do much of this work together. B.A. and I have been married for fifty-five years. The secret to making it work is giving in to my wife! It's very much different from the work I did in politics!!

Lloyd Bentsen

Peter Norton Software Entrepreneur and Gentleman Philanthropist

Homemaker and Philanthropist Eileen Norton

We met, had a drink, had dinner, and went to a bookstore to browse. I think we both felt we liked each other. The next day during my lunch break from work I found myself driving over to a local shopping mall and scouting through jewelry stores. I bought a modest necklace of freshwater pearls. As I was buying it, I was saying to myself, there is a message here. I've never done anything like this before. You don't normally do this after a first date. It was not an extravagant gift, but a string of pearls, no matter how cheap, is not the ordinary token after a first date. And I realized that the back of my head was sending a message to the front of my head. So, I gave her this little set of pearls and it has been onward and upward ever since.   **Peter Norton**

How did we meet? It was a singles ad if you really must know. We each had an ad in the paper. We made our date. It was love at first sight.

When we met in 1981, I was a teacher and Peter was a computer programmer. A few months later, Peter got one of IBM's first home personal computers. He lost some data on one of his disks and that's how the idea for Norton Utilities came to him. *Unerase* was a main program! The business really got started in spring '82. By June of '82, school was out and I started working for him full time. I was the gopher; went to the post office, to the hardware store—whatever errands he needed. We did everything from his kitchen table. Peter sat in his apartment in front of the computer, night and day, every day. He started selling his programs by mail and to users groups, clubs of enthusiasts in the early days. By the end of '82, he was going broke. By '83, things were looking up!

We started this business cranking out diskettes and thought it would be a nice little business and the two of us would have a job. Maybe we could buy a house and maybe we could have a couple of kids, but be very middle class. We had no idea that it would grow and grow by leaps and bounds.

Our marriage has been such a roller-coaster ride. Peter has a very wry sense of humor, and yes, I still laugh. There has never been a dull moment. We have been places and met people I would never have imagined. All these diskettes and books that were sold afford us a lifestyle that has enabled us to be charitable. We have a remarkable life.   **Eileen Norton**

Sheila Schafer Housewife

Entrepreneur Harold Schafer

Harold is a wonderful man . . . he's incredible because his memory of everything is so great. We were both born with an enormous amount of energy and we have a high level of enjoyment. We are kind to each other and we are romantic. I could write a book on everything Harold has thought of doing. I went bowling once and all the pins came down covered in pink carnations. He's thinking of something all the time.

He loves to give and do things for people. Harold could live on three or four hours of sleep, get up, shave, whistle, and hardly wait to go to work every day of his life. We are very appreciative and don't think that the good fortune that has come to us is something we earned; we just think we were blessed. Harold's given away more than he's ever earned, time and time and time again.

At one time there were no streets in Medora, no curbs, no gutters, no nothing. The first six or seven million came out of Harold's pocket. Everyone told him he was throwing his money away. Thirty years later Medora is the biggest tourist attraction in our state; it's very family oriented and people love it. Harold is going to be known more for Medora than the Gold Seal company, Snowy Bleach, or Mister Bubble.

We have eight wonderful children. One's the governor of North Dakota, and the others are fantastic, too. They are all associated with each other, and their children associate with each other. I am Harold's constant companion and constant champion. He's the most romantic person that ever lived, and the most generous. This was a man who was generous before he made money.

Sheila Schafer

Sheila was the wife of a very dear friend of mine. I danced with her at a dance one night, and at Thanksgiving a year later, I asked her husband if I got a divorce, could I marry his wife? My first wife and I separated, and Sheila's husband let her have a divorce. We got married.

We've been married twenty-five times over the course of thirty-one years. We have a renewal of the marriage vows often. All surprises! I lead her to the altar and she still accepts me. We were married in Christ Church in Long Island, in a church in Williamsburg, in the Notre Dame church in San Francisco, in an Orthodox church in Greece. We've been married at Wayfarer's Chapel in Los Angeles three or four times, including the first time.

Harold Schafer

Thomas Maino <small>Flight Surgeon</small>

<small>Flight Surgeon</small> Kimberly Maino

I used to be an engineer, but I wanted more meaning in my life, so I became a doctor. My family's always been pro-military, and the military gives you a great program for getting to medical school. So I probably would have gone into the military anyway.

My first impression of Kim was that she was pretty. Then when I got to know her, I found out she was fun. And then, throughout our internships, I realized she was a very smart doctor. I couldn't lose!

Our life is going to get real hard for the next five or six years, through our residencies. That's a tough lifestyle. After that, it will get a little easier, but we'll still be in the military, so it will continue to be demanding. My first goal is to become a board certified general surgeon and then the next big step will be to start a family. Those are the two big goals looming on the horizon.

We could be called into active duty anytime. My squadron is all packed up to deploy. It's not a day-to-day worry because that's the job we've trained to do, and we're ready to go, but still nobody wants to go to war. Ultimately, we'll probably settle in the Southeast somewhere. Kim likes the beach. I like the mountains. We'll go somewhere that gives us both.

Thomas Maino

I came from a military family. My father went to Vietnam and I was raised through that. My dad retired in the military. When I was in high school, I decided I wanted to serve my country. At that time, I was told one of the best ways to do it was to go to the Naval Academy. I was looking into careers women could have. I didn't think most of them would benefit me on the outside. Then I met a surgeon who opened my eyes and suggested medicine. I never dreamed I could be a doctor, but when I realized it could happen, I made it happen. The military paid for my college and my medical school. I owe them nine years in the military. We forget what the military has done for America because we haven't had a major war in a long time. The military has made us a vital part of what we are and what we're to be.

Tom and I were both surgery interns at Portsmouth Naval Academy. I was twenty-seven years old and he was four years older when we met. It was more of a friendship in the beginning. Tom is a great guy. He's a lot of fun. He's introduced me to things I thought I'd never do, like rock climbing, skiing, and scuba diving.

We're best friends who adore each other. He's someone I never thought I could find. I got way lucky. We take the risk of being separated. You realize you're taking that risk in the military, but if you have a strong marriage and a strong relationship, you should be able to work through it. The separation tests the relationship. Tom and I are lucky because we have the friendship that keeps it together.

Kimberly Maino

Bonnie Burkee Printmaker and Sculptor

Painter and Sculptor Irvin Burkee

At the onset, I knew Irv and I would have a unique life together. We were students at the Chicago Art Institute when we met in 1941. At the time I could not have conceived of leaving the establishment behind, leaving Chicago and living in the mountains.

We could have gone anywhere in the United States when we finished school, but there was no question in Irv's mind that we would go West. (At age twelve, he'd run away from home with his bicycle, a handmade trailer, and staples from his mother's pantry only to be apprehended at the Mississippi River, three hundred miles west of his Wisconsin home.) So, West we went!

Irv ingeniously thought of buying some raw property in the Rocky Mountains. There was no water and no electricity. We built a log cabin, fourteen by seventeen feet, and it was heaven. I asked Irv how we'd support ourselves, to which he responded, "I'll teach you how to make jewelry." For those eight years, in quite a limited area with a narrow workbench and a rather small number of tools, we were able to create a product which we could very easily ship to arts and crafts galleries all over the United States.

When our oldest child reached school age, we realized the quality of education in our small town was not adequate. We knew that our children deserved more scope than what was provided there, so we moved to a little town on the other side of Colorado called Aspen, which was beginning to grow. We built another house for ourselves there.

We've had four children. Both our daughters are artists. Our two sons died, one from complications from the red measles, and the other in an automobile accident. There's no way to ease the grief. Time can only help to cloak the tragedies.

Having the ability to focus on our artistic endeavors has been a rewarding ally in life. I don't think anything but creative expression in the art realm could have fulfilled us. Irv is a courageous man and going through life with him is an experience, no part of which I would ever change.

Bonnie Burkee

Our life together has been very complete. It is my idea of what a relationship should be, very closely knit. We spent a year together on my fellowship after we got out of school, and got used to being together every day. I decided that would be an ideal way to live.

It's a true union. We both have the same respect, attitude, and share almost all the same desires. I was twenty-seven when we got married and Bonnie was twenty-two. We were quite mature and I just wanted to be alone with her. The relationship grew more and more successful as time went by.

I was particularly attracted to Bonnie at the start because of her ability to be self-reliant, and she was beautiful. She was unusual. The chemistry just works when you meet the person that you want to live with for the rest of your life and it grows into a reality. What more could one ask? We wake up each morning as enthusiastic about each other as we've always been. We've been together for fifty-one years. It's more exciting now than it was at first. We are never bored.

Irvin Burkee

Los Gatos, California 1994

Fred Doelker Retired High School Teacher

Retired Cable Car and Bus Driver and Volunteer Santa Claus James Albee

Jimmy and I were in our thirties when we met. Jimmy's the one who talks. I don't talk. Normally, I don't care for people; I'm very quiet. I like to be by myself. Where we live now, we don't see too many people. I hate cocktail parties. I refuse to go to them. I freeze up and can't even eat. Jimmy's just the opposite; there's nobody he can't talk to.

A lot of people think it's strange that we always keep our lives together. We even went down and bought our burial plots together. We also paid for the funerals, so we won't leave trouble for the other one. The wills are all made out.

Sex isn't the main part of life. It's exciting and everything, but the friendship is more important than anything else. In the gay life there is bar hopping from bar to bar, and then what you call a trick. We never did that. A lot of the people we know are all gone with AIDS. It's all right to be gay, but live a normal life. Live together and help each other if you're sick. Help feed each other and have animals if you like them. Go out together, but always come home together. At our age now, we still respect each other. I guess you could call it love. I couldn't imagine a day without him. **Fred Doelker**

I was born in 1922 on Telegraph Hill in San Francisco. We were called "rock dwellers." Telegraph Hill was the low-income section of San Francisco because they had no transportation up there. There was no such thing as gas or electricity on the Hill. During the Depression, everybody was out of work. People were hungry. The goat woman used to come around with a flock of goats; you'd give her five cents and she'd milk a goat and you'd drink it down. The trains didn't have refrigeration cars, so we always came home with ten, fifteen, twenty potatoes. My mother used to wash the potato sacks after we ate the potatoes, turn them around and make little pants or skirts out of them. My dad worked as a fireman on a fireboat along the piers, near the railroad tracks. I was always walking there.

As I got older, Telegraph Hill became expensive. I was just finishing high school when the war came along. My dad told me to go into the army or navy, and to go into the cooking department. You never go hungry! So I joined the navy and spent five years as a cook. After the navy, I started to work on the cable cars when the fare was five cents.

When I drove the bus, I used to stop it at Steiner and Union. That's where Fred got on. Every time I saw him standing there, I always stopped in front of him to make sure that he could get on. One Saturday evening, we happened to run into each other in a gay bar. Fred didn't run around much. I didn't run around much. He invited me to dinner, and I invited him back to dinner.

I don't know how I figured out I was gay. I just didn't care for women, had no desire for women. It was hard to find somebody that you could share a home with. Fred and I are like husband and wife. Fred takes care of the money and the house. He decides where we go and what we do. We don't have arguments. We're together forty years this year.

James Albee

Renee Bristol Restaurant Owner

Restaurant Owner Jason Sarisky

I knew Jason when I was a little kid. He lived right behind me. He used to carry my grandmother's groceries for her. We have our whole childhood in common. It's neat.

We've been together for five years, but we're not married. In Jason's eyes, a marriage license is just a piece of paper. He's happy we're together and planning for us to be together forever. Marriage is a bigger deal for me. I'm the traditional woman who wants to have a wedding.

We wanted to get married this summer, but we were too busy. I worked from sunrise to sunset, and he worked another job in addition to this job. We never had a day off. We worked so much to try to get the restaurant going, we hardly had time to sleep. We bought the business the day after my twentieth birthday. You learn a lot about each other when you live and work together. Overall, it's been a wonderful experience. I wouldn't go back or change the decision to work and make choices together. Jason has been very supportive. I couldn't have done it without him and he couldn't have done it without me.

Jason knows what he wants. He's twenty-four years old. He's brilliant. I admire him. Sometimes he's a little strong and dominating, but that's just the male in him. There aren't many people like that out there who have such goals. When he wants something, he does it. I'm not like that. I let things get in the way sometimes, but nothing stops Jason. We're learning to enjoy each other.

Renee Bristol

I was born and raised in Livingston, Montana. I met Renee when I was getting out of high school, she was about fifteen. Renee is very energetic and very friendly. She's too trusting. Maybe I don't trust people so much because I used to be a police officer. Renee is willing to help anyone out. She's a loving and caring person. She's family oriented.

I see that we'll probably have children. We'll try to be simple. Doing things together is more important than being prosperous. This business has taught us that time is more important than anything and there's not very much of it. We'll spend time together and not worry about money. If things happen, they happen, if not, they don't. We don't want to be famous or rich. We don't want to ruin our personal life over that kind of pursuit.

Jason Sarisky

Joan Ankrum <small>Retired Art Dealer</small>

<small>Retired Businessman</small> Robert Baumgarten

One day in 1992 I was surprised to find my answering machine had the message, "This is Bob Baumgarten. We haven't seen each other for sixty years. I'd like to see you and find out what you've been up to."

Stunned, I didn't reply til two days later. After all, we had been sweethearts when he was twenty, and I sixteen, and we were in love. We had even won a silver cup dancing the Charleston at the St. Francis Hotel in San Francisco. But we had parted, each pursuing different goals, he in finance and business, and I in theater and art.

Now I called him back, saying, "Come over and I'll tell you." So he did, and our reunion was magical, and we've been together ever since.

Joan Ankrum

In December 1992 I found my love of 1928, whom I hadn't seen since my student days in Palo Alto. I called Joan to arrange a meeting. We promised we wouldn't say to each other, "You haven't changed a bit. You haven't, have you?"

"Yes," she said. "I'm wiser."

On her eightieth birthday I sent her flowers with a note:

"To a beautiful girl who became a lovely, charming, accomplished woman almost overnight."

So now here we are, happy and in love again, together for the rest of our lives, as we were fated to be.

Robert Baumgarten

Lynne Seus Wolf Trainer

Bear Trainer Doug Seus

I literally ran into Doug. He was going in one door of a restaurant and I was going out the other. Sparks flew. The cosmos happened. That was in 1969. He was so weird. He was the most unique man I'd ever met. On our first date he took me to feed a rhino viper, to watch the second most deadly snake in the world eat a rat. He was into herpetology at the time. I thought to myself, whatever it will be, it will never be boring. That has proved to be true.

Doug is consumed by a passion. He is the best bear trainer in the world. He has a certain ability and magic with those animals that I don't think has ever been before or will be again. It doesn't come easy. You have to have not only the talent, but the dedication and perseverance. In the times when we were auditioning for a film and Bart the bear required a new behavior, like teaching him to limp, Doug was able to accomplish it in just a few days. But those few days were intense. He didn't have time for anything or anyone else.

Doug is guileless, incapable of acting any other way than he truly feels, brutally honest, and always real. I think that's why he's so incredibly good with animals, because animals demand that from you. You can't be anything other than one hundred percent real. They'll call you on any insincere feeling. He's one in a million. It's a grand adventure.   **Lynne Seus**

Lynne is the stalwart of the family. She always holds things together. She's got stamina, stands by anybody and anything through thick and thin. Without a good woman, you're never going to make it. She's been my wife and my best friend for thirty years.

I have a tyrannical madness when it comes to Bart. Because of my obsessive nature and tunnel vision personality in acquiring perfection in my work, I always put Bart first. I've put Lynne through so much. I'm lucky to still have her.

There are people in the world who are bear people. Working with bears is a natural gift. I'll spend an enormous amount of hours with them because I enjoy it. I'm not a particularly patient person. I'm persistent. That's passion. You can learn technique, but the timing is intuitive and critical. You're born with a sense of timing. Training an animal is an art form if done properly—fluid and beautiful. It's abusive and archaic if you work with an animal in the wrong way.

Lynne, Bart, and I made our business a success together. Lynne and I have the same interests; we like history and are in awe of the natural world. Bart's an extension of our passion and has enabled us to make this a better world through our work with the environment. He bought the first ranch for his wild brothers and gave it back to them. Lynne is my best friend and my love. Bart is my soul.   **Doug Seus**

Harriet Beinfield Acupuncturist and Author

Chinese Medicine Doctor Efrem Korngold

Efrem and I met on the Black Bear Ranch commune in northern California in 1969. There were sixty of us who lived on the commune as an extended family. We had grown out of the Diggers, who were some of the early founders of what later became known as the Flower Children. Efrem and I first came together in the middle of the wilderness in a conversation about Doris Lessing. I felt as if we were tribal siblings. Efrem doesn't exist on the surface; his interior shines in the moonlight. We had a similar picture of the world and how we wanted to be in it.

We went to a one-week seminar on Chinese medicine and we were seized with a magnetic sense that we knew what we wanted to do next. In 1972, we went to England to study Chinese medicine. I was seduced by the poetry and the philosophy of it. I had finally found a way for all my interests to come together. I could be a doctor like my dad and grand-dads, and also study a way of thinking that seemed to portray a different world, the world of the body. For his own reasons, Efrem was equally interested in the pursuit of Chinese medicine. We soon found there weren't enough people who needed our help in the woods, so we moved to San Francisco and studied with a Chinese teacher, traveling to England and to China.

We had a son twenty-one years ago who was born with two big holes in his heart. We were isolated from the normal world of healthy people, because when you have a sick child you are not like everybody else. It ignited something in me that was pre-existing before our son's birth—a deep and abiding interest in human suffering, what its meaning is, and how to live in the face of it. Efrem and I are bonded by that interest.   **Harriet Beinfield**

I spent a great deal of my early life alone. I envied my friends who had siblings. Brothers and sisters who love and care about each other often wrestle, like it's a serious thing, but it's also a form of intimacy that produces great intensity and satisfaction. Harriet and I dare each other to do certain things or think certain ways, and it becomes a kind of sibling contest. That way of relating is a quality of our relationship, and it's partly how we egg each other on to be creative. I didn't realize at first that it was simply a way of relating, not necessarily an attempt to win or lose.

Relationships in which people try to submerge their differences for the sake of "the harmony of the relationship" often fall apart because of the result of that abnegation; sacrifice, losing yourself, squashing yourself. That's what parents do to children. The parent is often the dominant and important figure and the child learns that in order to be loved, he or she must become the field on which the parent can project him or herself. The child tries to take on the parent's issues, desires, problems, and needs, and they become lost; they never find out who they are.

Harriet has a talent for creating a family more than any person I have ever met. She has helped me create a family and I appreciate that about her more than anything. She's my equal in all respects, intellectually and socially. We have struggled ardently with each other from the very beginning, but we seem to be complementary; she has skills that I don't have and I have skills that she doesn't have. We seem to be made for each other. Our life together hasn't always been easy. I don't even know that it's easy now, but it is never boring because I am infinitely curious about Harriet, and take great pleasure in just watching her live her life. Way down deep, we not only love each other, but find one another fascinating. We really and truly want the other person to be happy; to get what they want and what they need in this life. Whether we can necessarily provide it or not is another issue. But the desire, the intent, is fundamental.   **Efrem Korngold**

Thomas Daniel Restaurant Manager
Guest Services Manager Barbara Webster

I got into the restaurant business as a bartender and waiter, and then I became a manager. Barbara came into the restaurant and tried to sell me cellular phones. I wasn't interested in the phones, but we had a cup of coffee. . . .

The interracial aspect of our relationship doesn't play any role at all for me. Some people are so silly. People are just people. Actually, Barbara and I are opposite in a lot of ways. She's a Democrat. I'm a Republican. I'm a Celtics fan. She's a Lakers fan. We were on different sides in the O. J. Simpson trial. To a point I understand where she's coming from. Not having walked in those shoes I could never understand what it's really like. I mean, look at me. I'm as Anglo-Saxon as they get. Cabs always pick me up, I never get a stare, I get seated at nice tables at restaurants. I'm not making a huge comment on the United States, but it is true that that sort of thing does happen. When I see a police car I think positively about the officers; they put their life on the line every day. I don't tense up.

Even though we're different in some areas, we live and let live pretty well. We are accepting of each other. That's the best thing we've got going. Barbara doesn't have a nagging bone in her body. For three straight months she got up at four o'clock every morning and drove me to work when my car was on the fritz and we were saving for a house. She did it with a smile on her face every day. I don't know if I could do that!

We're really happy that we are going to be with each other. We reckon that we will work hard for the next twenty years and be able to enjoy life a little bit as we go along too. We're not putting pressure on ourselves for children. We're just taking care of each other right now. **Thomas Daniel**

I need someone who is understanding, respectable, and lets me be independent. Tom gives that to me. Tom is the first Anglo-American who is in my family. I come from a military family and I grew up in predominately all-white neighborhoods, so I don't feel any difference, black and white or colored, nor does my family. They have taken him in as Tom. On the other hand, Tom's family is trying to adjust and adapt to the relationship.

We own a home, a garden home with lots of flowers—tulips—and we have herbs, and tomatoes, vegetables. Tom is a gardener. I never knew that. I was lucky to get someone who has a green thumb. I am in the kitchen, and keep the house nice and neat. We are going to fix up the house and sell it, get a bigger home later. Or who knows? A beach house. That is my ultimate dream. **Barbara Webster**

Mark Adams Artist

Artist Beth Van Hoesen

This photograph brings forth all sorts of things we had never fathomed before. There's something about an illness in a relationship that puts a responsibility on both people. On the one hand, one person has to assume responsibilities that he didn't have before. And on the other hand, the one who is ill assumes the responsibility of guilt. We both have a role to play and I don't think either one is easy. It's very difficult for anyone who has been independent all their life to suddenly be put in the position of not being independent. It's difficult to sit there and accept what the other is doing for you. It's hard to depend on someone else for everything. Our relationship has become much, much richer since this happened. No one who gets married thinks it will happen, but we love each other even more now.   **Mark Adams**

We may paint the same object, but Mark finds the archetypical rose and I find the one with worms and holes in it. What I care about most, whether it's an animal, a person, or a leaf, is that it must be individualistic and it must be alive and different. Individualistic is what I care for. But I'm always interested in what he sees.

There are so many artists who marry and don't get along because their ideas are different. There were times when it would be very difficult for me to walk through Mark's studio when he was working on something without wanting to criticize it or correct it. We made a pact that we wouldn't criticize each other's work until we were asked. It worked very well, but I couldn't look at his work when I walked through the studio because I'd get opinions!

We never had children, not that we didn't want them. If we had, we wouldn't have been able to spend so much time on art. I know if we'd had a child, the child would have come first. We were very fortunate that we had the time and seemed to make just enough money to take trips to Europe which we could not afford now. We also went to India, North Africa, Egypt, Bora Bora, many places. If you're an artist, it's a full-time job. For us, the artworks are our children and we hope they go to good homes. We've had a marvelous life together.

Beth Van Hoesen

Al Hirschfeld Artist

Theater Historian Louise Kerz Hirschfeld

Reverend Ethan Acres Minister and Artist

Student Nurse Lisa Acres

Lisa is the most profoundly interesting soul I've ever met. It goes beyond gender. She's bright and fun and sparkly and everything I'd dreamed Vegas would be. At times, I thought I was drowning and didn't know what I'd do with my life. Lisa made me stronger. She has a calming effect on me. I feel better about everything when I'm with her.

I grew up in northeastern Alabama and my mom married a very charismatic, hellfire-and-brimstone Baptist circuit minister. Albert, as a child, had lost his arms. He'd climbed what he thought was a telephone line, but it was actually a high-tension power line and he was electrocuted. That's when he saw God and received his calling. He had the greatest influence on my life and that affects my life with Lisa.

When I was eleven, we had a little, rust-eaten Toyota Corolla that we used to take from church to church. One hot summer Sunday, we were going as fast as we could to the next church. Albert suddenly realized that his prosthetic arms had locked up on the steering wheel. We pulled into that little church and he was so angry. Suddenly, Albert turned to me in the backseat and said, "Son, I want you to take that knife I gave you, boy, and I want you to reach up under my robe and cut the straps off these arms." He went in that church and preached that sermon without any arms. I'll never forget the image of Albert flying around on the pulpit in his black robe without his arms. It's an image of leaving behind that thing that separates us from other people. Every person in that church got up and came to the front at the end of that day and, praise God, it was the most incredible religious experience that I ever had. It was funny and powerful all wrapped up into one. I decided then and there I wanted to be a minister.

Where I grew up, Vegas was the Devil's playground if there ever was one. The first thing I saw when I came here were two Elvis impersonators walking up the sidewalk, holding hands at four-thirty in the morning. The pathetic weirdness of Vegas touched me profoundly. It was a place that so desperately wanted to be something more. To build a town like this in the middle of the desert makes no sense whatsoever, but the poetic beauty of it trying, affected me. I got on the phone to Lisa and said, "Darling, we're moving to Vegas." By the time I got home a few days later, that woman had packed up the truck. It was a testament of her love for me.

Ethan Acres

I met Ethan in an art class at Mississippi Gulf Coast Community College. I'd just turned eighteen when I met him. Ethan had big baby cheeks and long hair; he was tall and good looking. He was extremely friendly, down to earth, and generous with his time and attention.

Ethan took the Bible study courses necessary to become an ordained minister. Then we moved to Vegas. We built the highway chapel soon after we got here. Ethan quotes Isaiah 43 as saying, "Make straight in the desert a highway for your God." He thinks it's a fitting verse for Vegas, the idea of building something more. We bought a 1965 Shasta trailer from a sweet Mexican family. They were keeping goats and chickens in it, so it smelled horrible, but the shape was so beautiful, Ethan just ignored the dung. It's egg shaped, a solid white chapel with Bible verses and a church facade on the side. It has stained-glass windows and neon beneath, so at night it glows. It looks like it lifts off the ground. It's in front of our house. Ethan preaches a lot to the homeless in the street. It's not an organized congregation, but more of an outreach program.

We've lived together for eight years and been married for three. We didn't have a lot of money to pay for our wedding. We got married at the Graceland Wedding Chapel. For a little extra, we got an Elvis impersonator to perform at our wedding, so Elvis was singing as my father walked me down the aisle. It was a very nice ceremony, short but filled with emotion.

Ethan and I have a really great relationship. We have total trust in each other and total love for each other. I don't know what I'd do without him. I wouldn't want to give him up.

Lisa Acres

Anne Armstrong Former Ambassador

Rancher Tobin Armstrong

My husband is extremely male, which I like. He has more common sense and good judgment than anybody else I've ever met. He's an extremely balanced person. He has lots of hobbies. He loves many things, from his family to his work to his heritage, and he has forward vision, too. It couldn't be a better marriage for romantic love, companionship, for guidance. He can handle any situation. I can get excited, lose my temper, or get scared, but Tobin's always in control. If I had to search the world over for another husband, even now with almost fifty years of experience, I'd go right back and find Tobin Armstrong. **Anne Armstrong**

Anne and I had known each other casually through our families. I brought her down to the ranch after a weekend party in the Davis Mountains. I had it in my mind to persuade her that this might not be a bad place to come and live. My aunt and uncle, who lived here, were an extraordinarily attractive couple and I think that was part of the charm of this place that appealed to Anne. I didn't waste any time proposing to her. She had been thinking seriously of working in New York, but I told her that if she took the job there, I wouldn't be able to run back and forth to pursue her, no matter how much I'd like to. She changed her mind and decided she would marry me and come and live here. Giving her that ultimatum was the smartest thing I ever did!

Anne entered into life on the ranch with complete enthusiasm. We started off from scratch. She took over the bookkeeping, worked the cattle with me, and mastered the ranching business in every sense. We lived in a little three-room cottage, but immediately added on to make it comfortable. We had a family started within a year and a half and had five children before the oldest one was five years old. That tells you something about how many different activities there were down here!

After the kids got big enough to go off to boarding school, Anne involved herself in politics. She zoomed right up to the top of the Republican Party and worked with four presidents. Anne is remarkably bright and a very feeling, sensitive, concerned person. She has a clearly defined sense of values, a wonderful sense of humor, and a great appreciation for the serious and the fun things in life. She has a vast amount of energy; she's a tireless worker and a hard-driving achiever; a communicator of extraordinary capacity beyond anything I've seen anywhere. Her interests are sincere.

Tobin Armstrong

Mike Wallace Journalist

Former Television Producer Mary Yates Wallace

Mike and I have been friends for more than forty years, and then bingo, one day we decided to marry. Now we wonder why we waited so long.　　**Mary Yates Wallace**

New Orleans, Louisiana 1998

John Minor Wisdom United States Judge, Fifth Circuit Court of Appeals

Housewife Bonnie Wisdom

In my most important school case, the Jefferson case, and later in the Meredith case, I said there's got to be "affirmative action to integrate." I was the first to use that verbiage. I took the position that the Constitution is not only color-blind, but it is also color conscious. It is color-blind to prevent discrimination and color conscious to rectify previous discrimination.

Most of my friends did not agree with me, but we've never lost a friend because of my legal actions. Many people did not like what I did because most people in New Orleans, like most people in the South, were very strongly segregationist. I felt strongly that the law required the courts to provide equality in accordance with the Constitution. Others would agree to equality according to the Constitution, but defined that in terms of inaction.

Bonnie is a highly intelligent girl. She is independent, and strongly assertive of any position she takes on important matters. That is fine with me, even though at times we may disagree. She has an enormous interest in and knowledge of Shakespeare and Mozart, as well as a tremendous ability to recite poems that she's learned. Bonnie cannot sing, but she has a better ability to identify a strain of good music than anyone else I know. She doesn't like to cook, but she is an extraordinarily good cook, with the rare knack for the ability to identify all the ingredients of a good sauce or salad. Bonnie has an unusually fine knowledge of good literature and is quick at repartee. For me it has been fun and a pleasure, challenging and exhilarating for all the sixty-seven years of our marriage.   **John Minor Wisdom**

I grew up on a large sugar plantation. My great-grandfather had been the presiding judge of the first Louisiana Supreme Court. When we bought Louisiana in 1806, he had come down to be a territorial judge. They were Virginians before that. I was taught at home and I think I learned about everything I know now by the age of ten. After that, I boarded at a small school in New Orleans until I went to Sweet Briar College.

John and I can't remember where we met each other, but we think it was a Trinity Church Sunday School picnic when I was still in high school. People in New Orleans who more or less move around in the same circles just more or less meet each other one way or another. It was my senior year at Sweet Briar that my husband began to court me seriously. I thought he was very intelligent, very attractive and a good dancer. I liked him.

I have my own interests. I have done a lot of work in the Elizabethan field. It's quite stimulating and it's interesting to have a milieu you can move into like the Elizabethan period when you want to get out of this present time.

Unlike my husband, I have no knowledge of the law. Do you remember the Father William poem?

> . . . you swallowed the goose bold beak and all
> Pray, how did you manage to do it?
> In my youth, he replied, I studied the law
> And I argued each case with my wife
> And the muscular strength that it gave to my jaw
> Has lasted the rest of my life.

That, I've always thought, was a very sensible approach to avoid. I did not want to be like the wife of Father William, so I don't argue the law and I don't know anything about it.

John is an excellent bridge player, exceedingly difficult to get along with at the bridge table, to the extent that one time after a battle, I said, "I'm never going to play with you again." And guess what, I never have!   **Bonnie Wisdom**

Maya Lin Architect and Artist
Art Dealer Daniel Wolf

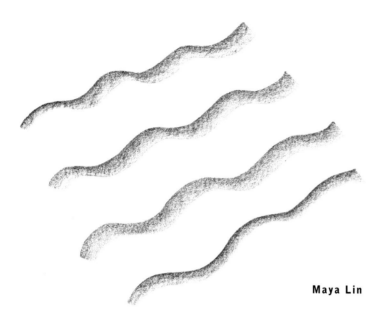

Maya Lin

We knew each other for a while. When we fell in love, it was like a tidal wave came over us. It was as if something came out of the water, lifted us up, and sent us soaring. It hasn't stopped.

Daniel Wolf

LIST OF PORTRAITS